D1702134

THE

BREAK-FREE MESSAGE

Guidance by a Spiritual Master

KALINDI

Miracle of Love

THE BREAK-FREE MESSAGE:
Guidance by a Spiritual Master

© 2008 Miracle of Love®

First Edition, 2008

Published by Miracle of Love
4277 W. 43rd Avenue
Denver, CO 80212

*All rights reserved. No part of this book may be reproduced
in any form or stored in a retrieval system, transmitted,
or reproduced in any way including but not limited to photocopy,
magnetic or other means, without prior permission
in writing from the publisher.*

*Please note that Miracle of Love®, Path to Ultimate Freedom®,
The Intensive®, Modern-Day Meditation®, GMP®,
Gourasana Meditation Practice®, and Meditation for This Age®
are all registered trademarks of Miracle of Love®.*

Library of Congress Control number: 2008934188

ISBN 978-1-892546-07-4

Printed in Canada

We are pleased that you have purchased *The Break-Free Message* and offer our gratitude for your interest. We trust that you will find Kalindi's words both inspirational and helpful in your endeavor to come closer to God's love and truth. We hope that you find great benefit from this book, that it alters your consciousness positively, and that it supports you to have a long, God-conscious life.

Kalindi's guidance is meant for healthy people of sound mind who want to come closer to God. If you choose to follow Kalindi's spiritual guidance, we urge you to do so responsibly and with full love, care, and respect for yourself and others – as that is one of Kalindi's core teachings.

Definitions of names and terms used throughout this book can be found at the back of the book.

For my blessed Gourasana,
"The Golden One"

Having found You in 1987
and been blessed countless times by You
all the way into a full state
of awareness and the endless love of God,
I dedicate this book and every
word I speak to You, my Lord.
For without You, Your words of truth
and love would have never pierced my heart
to the point of speaking the truth
that can guide one to ultimate freedom.
To You, I offer myself
again and again.

KALINDI

*The only thing people
really care about, truly care about,
is the love of God.
The thing they want more than
anything is love.
And without that connection to God,
they can't have the feeling of love
they really want.
There is nothing greater.
There is nothing
more important to each and
every human being
than love.
It is everything.*

❧

God's love is for everyone.

GOURASANA

CONTENTS

"I'm here to take you Home."

KALINDI

On Breaking Free

I welcome you and hope these words of spiritual guidance are of assistance to you in your spiritual journey and awakenings.

The Break-Free Message contains my main condensed teachings, though volumes of books on various topics have been spoken. *Breaking free* refers to breaking free from the binding force of illusion, which is anything and everything that causes one to be or feel separate from God, self, and others. In that sense, this guidance can be of assistance to anyone going through serious transformation to return to – or to be in closer relationship with – God in the highest.

The Break-Free Message is a collection of my core teachings that are specific for someone who is on the path to break the cycle of birth and death. This is addressing those of you who have the desire to break free in this lifetime, no rebirth – all the way Home to the arms of the Almighty. This is addressing those who are ready to find the true meaning of full enlightenment.

These specific teachings were of utmost importance to my disciples' spiritual success in achieving full awareness and breaking the cycle of birth and death. I am happy the words came out of my mouth; many people have now become advanced spiritual masters who can help others in the awakening process. That is why these talks have been compiled, because if you are in rapid spiritual transformation, you will probably need these words for step-by-step guidance. This book is invaluable.

The talks are about the subject of breaking free of the ego and the process that it takes each step of the way. The first lesson of this teaching begins *now*, and that has to do with understanding that the core of *The Break-Free Message* is based on one very simple and unavoidable fact. This fact is that you can't sit around waiting for someone else to do your spiritual work for you. No matter how much help you get on your spiritual journey, *if you don't do your part, you will not make it all the way.*

Of course, it's okay if you don't make it all the way Home to God, no rebirth in this lifetime, because you will make it Home eventually. Everyone does. It is just a matter of timing, evolution and desire. But for someone who wants to make it *in their current lifetime*, it is not okay to labor under the misconception that spiritual freedom can or will only happen by following a concept – in your mind, or in a doctrine, or in a single practice. Some people try to find God by a kind of waiting, or by thinking that enlightenment will happen by "willing it to happen" or by "having a positive attitude" or something like that. These are misconceptions in contemporary spiritual life.

It is my desire that those of you who are serious about wanting to be with God understand that to break free requires something other than waiting, wishing, hoping, or expecting. You can't wait for something to happen so you can have spiritual movement. You have to create the spiritual movement by looking at your illusions through a magnifying glass. You have to scrutinize yourself to find out what is binding you. You have to do that work; and I know of no softer way to say it.

Anyone who gets completely free from the illusion finds the true meaning of enlightenment, and they have to let go of so much while they are in good enough physical health and mobility before the limitations of old age set in. Then when it comes time to prepare for death, there is so much more of a very different nature that one has to go through. That is why *urgency* and *action* are at the core of this teaching. There simply is no time to procrastinate. I do belabor this point because it is at the heart of my teachings – you cannot for one minute, not for one day, give up on your effort to want to be fully with God. And it is not enough to just want to be fully with God. The ongoing thought *behind every other thought* has to be something like "I don't want to take birth again" or "I'm going all the way Home to God."

You have to approach your spiritual life with unshakable determination and, of course, there is also calm and peace inside. It's not like you are a raving lunatic on your spiritual path, but you have to get some determination going that is way outside of your comfort zone, because you have one constant enemy, and that is the illusion. Every single person, in some way, is bound by the illusion. The illusion is the force that is constantly after you. Those on a spiritual path to God must be picking away at that force constantly, and with the sheer power of will, making it get away from them. You have to see the illusion, then you have to pray, then you have got to act, and make changes. No one can understand how much they are going to have to get through in order to have full union with God.

The true spiritual path is one where you work away at your illusion until it is worn down. You just work away at it as if you are polishing a mirror, wiping off the dirt as it slowly begins to shine. That is an analogy to what spiritual work is like. Let yourself receive the joy and ecstasy of the path, and anything that feels good, if and when it comes to you, but otherwise you are serious and sober and you are going for full freedom. I am often up day and night just thinking about this, knowing that if the serious seekers would truly understand this message, they would for sure make it all the way Home.

These basic teachings are something that you must come to realize. They are something to guide you and to hold you in your endeavors as you transform, as you break freer and freer every day and come closer and closer to the love of God. I want to make these teachings very, very clear, because when you are doing this kind of work, going within in this type of way, you can become so lost in so many ways. You can become so stuck for years and years working on

2. Abs. The True spiritual path

issues, wallowing about so many things, and getting stuck in areas that you just need to let go of.

My words are just guidance to point you in the right direction. If the truth could be put into words and written in a book, then there would be a whole lot of people already free. It is so hard to guide people, to tell people, "Do it this way. Do it like this," because every person is so different, and it is impossible to explain the truth; it is impossible. All that can be done is to give guidance.

Spiritual guidance changes according to time, according to humankind's evolution. The guidance that I am bringing now is what humankind needs for what is going on right now in evolution; it is for people who are ready in their evolution to move forward right now and for the next era in time, the many, many centuries to come. As humankind evolves, a different kind of guidance will need to come – much later in time. But right now for the world, and heavily in the Western World, there are thousands of people ready to hear this kind of spiritual guidance. For the people who are ready to go Home, whether it is in this lifetime, or three or four or five or six lifetimes, my *Break-Free Message* is the guidance that needs to be heard. It needs to be heard in its entirety brought by a spiritual master who has the power and special assistance coming in from God that can help people break free.

The guidance alone can only get you so far. Without the special assistance coming in from God in this period of

You just need to let go

time (and that will continue to be here for many centuries to come) you cannot make it to full enlightenment. There are a few that are so advanced who will make it. There are always a few who can make it, but that is very, very rare.

So without a spiritual master with the power and the special assistance that is coming in from God right now, without the help, without the association of others who are doing the spiritual work, without the support system, you cannot make it all the way to union with God. The transformation that needs to happen right now is tumultuous; you have to remain so steadfast in your transformation. You cannot really let up on yourself at all.

You have to find your path, find your master, and stick to it. It is a long process.

Read *The Break-Free Message* many, many times over, because you will forget what has been said. Get into the habit of reading or listening* to it once a week or once every other week. Read the whole thing, because you will forget; as He starts pushing you and you start going through internal change, you will easily forget.

Godspeed in your transformation. The world needs you.

Kalindi

---

* *The Break-Free Message* is also available in audio format at *www.miracle.org*.

LET GO OF YOUR EGO

*Your true self will take over to
the degree that you let go of your
illusory self. It is that simple.
But to become enlightened is the
hardest thing, because instead
of dying and being reborn back
into the illusion – which you
are familiar with, because you
have been doing it for millions
of lifetimes – you are actually
dying to the entire illusion, and
you are entering into the realm
of God while you are alive.*

GOURASANA

What Is the Ego?

By The Lady

> We are using the word "ego" to mean false self, false personality. This must die for your true self, your true personality to live. Presently, your true self is lost and your false self is dominant. GOURASANA

It is only through the death of the ego that it is possible for the true self to become dominant. The ego dies in stages. As the ego is dying, your true self begins to awaken and attain union with God, because true self realization and God realization happen simultaneously. The fire of spiritual transformation forces you to let go of the ego – the false self, the separate self, the illusory self, the false personality. Spiritual transformation is the way to become free of the bondage of repeated births and deaths: reincarnation. Therefore to become free, to return Home to God, true self manifestation must occur while you are alive.

If by the time of your death, you do not succeed in true self manifestation with its accompanying union with God, you will take birth again. Illusory desires, judgments, concepts, beliefs, and attachments of the ego are some of the

Notes: *Illusory desires*
was 2nd ... illusory desires

causes for rebirth. When you take birth again, you basically continue in your next life where you left off in the last life. Whatever illusions that were binding you at the time of death will have to be dealt with in future lives, until all illusion is dispelled. In each life you are born into a different illusory personality and into different circumstances. This evolution continues until you want God and your true self more than the false self.

*

From awareness you will understand that the ego is neither good nor bad, it is just false.

> Whether you are moral or immoral, it is still just a part of the illusion. It must all be given up. If you think you are a very good person or a very bad person or something in between, it is all illusion and must go. Who you truly are is neither very good nor bad. You are something beyond duality. You are something beyond illusion.
>
> GOURASANA

People commonly strive to become better people by improving the false self. They mistakenly equate that improvement with spiritual advancement. This is a misconception and a cause for rebirth. Gourasana explains:

> People want to take the illusory self and have that illusory self come to a state of full awareness and become

Notes: To become a better person is not glide spiritual advancement misconception → a cause for rebirth

enlightened, but that is not possible. The illusory self cannot become enlightened, because it is an illusion. All that can happen to the illusory self is that it can disappear. That is why you must let go of who you think you are. Once you begin to let go of the illusion – of who you think you are – you will truly enter into the light, more and more. The illusion will disappear and you will come to know your true self.

The heart of spiritual transformation is to do what you need to do to let go of your illusory personality so your true self can take you over. It is no easy task. Until then, you think your illusory personality is you, because you have identified with and experienced millions of illusory selves in millions of lives.

*

Most people choose to stay in the plane of illusion. And even people that want to leave don't realize that the ego has a whole strategy to make sure the false self continues to exist. While addressing the question, "Is everyone going to get free?" Gourasana explains:

> You have to understand something about the illusion. All the illusion wants to do is make sure that you don't get free in this lifetime, so if it can't get you to stop this work, then its next objective is going to be to slow you

Notes: The heart of spiritual transformation is to do what you need to do to let go of your illusory personality.

down. Because if it can slow you down enough, then you won't be able to get free in this lifetime, and then it can deal with you in the next lifetime and use whatever tricks it is going to use in the next lifetime to capture you. So going back to the question: Is everyone going to get free? The reality is that everyone is not, because the illusion is going to slow you down enough so you just won't have enough time to make it. It's going to slow you down just enough, so move as quickly as you can. You see, the ego has a whole strategy going on to make sure that it continues and *you* do not make it. The ego tailors its strategy to you specifically.

So become aware. Keep up the momentum of your transformation. Turn your back on the illusion, walk away, and never look back.

The illusion always creates "good" excuses for not doing the work of transformation. There is never a right or convenient time to do your spiritual work. The situation is actually urgent. The only time you truly have, after all, is the present. So start now, keep going, and never give up.

*

A key to doing the work of quickly letting go of your ego is desire. Whenever you feel that you lack desire or your desire is weak, that is the time to pray for more desire. Pray-

Notes: *The ego tailors its strategy to you specifically.*
The ego has a whole strategy.
Please help me to see it.
Pray for more desire!

ing for more desire activates the energy and motion of desire. God responds to your desire. You can never use the excuse of not having enough desire. Gourasana tells us:

> Your desire, your true self, must be stronger than your ego. As strong as the ego is, it is desire that will save you. Desire is everything. If you desire the love and the light, then you *will* get it. Nothing will stand in your way if your desire is strong enough. You will begin to act and take the necessary steps to succeed. You can let your desire grow. There are ways to increase your desire.

*

If you sincerely want your true self and God, then you will take action now and do your part one hundred percent. Replace your procrastination and laziness with a sense of urgency. You only have now to find God, and only with God is the illusion defeated. *Pray for God to help you.* Pray to the Lord with your head at His feet to help you let go of your ego and your personality.

A Saint prays:
Please take all of me, Lord,
The good and the evil, the caring and the selfish;
The generous and the greedy, the kind and the mean;
The gentle and the harsh, the attractive and the ugly;

Notes: *Pray to the Lord with your head at His feet to help you let go of your ego and your personality*

The controlled and the addicted, the compassionate
and the cruel;
The perfect and the flawed, the innocent and the
shamed.
Please take all of me, Lord; I want nothing else but You.

*

In the following chapters, Kalindi gives information critical to becoming free of illusion and ego. She dissects
and exposes the illusion and ego from every angle, and she
teaches how to authentically do the work. It is critical to
listen to Kalindi. If you truly listen, then you will also act
upon her guidance. The work of how to get free of the illusion
and ego is no longer a mystery. There are no more excuses.

Good luck.

Just do it.

Never give up.

With love.

Notes:

You Are Not That Being of Illusion

Spoken on April 5, 2007

There is a main point that is critical to understand in your transformation while studying the Break-Free Message. You may not be able to actually understand it, but you need to be aware of it. The point is that, as you are working on yourself in your transformation, you need to know that you are not who you think you are. You are not that being of illusion in any way, shape or form – not at all.

You are not who you think you are. You are not that mind with all of its desires. You are not that body with all of its desires. You are not any part except that spirit that lies within, that returns Home. That spirit that returns Home takes nothing with it. Everything is completely let go of, and the body is the last thing that is let go of when you die. You are not a man. You are not a woman. Your uncle Harry is not going to be in Heaven waiting for you somewhere – it's not like that.

You have been away from your Home for so many lifetimes that you cannot even remember that there is such

Notes: Identification mit Body, mit Wünschen / mind

a thing as Home. You cannot remember at all who you are. And you think that you are all of the things that you have conjured up in your mind, these roles that you are living out in this lifetime. But you are just living out things, learning lessons, living things through, having a lifetime and then another lifetime and another lifetime until you let go of the being of illusion.

In the seminars we offer, what goes on is that a lot of the being of illusion is removed, and that is why you can feel so much more of a true part of yourself and your connection to God. In those seminars, so much of the illusion has been removed through your hard work and your letting go. And then some of you go right back and hang on to the illusion again – and that's too bad. But that is the power of the illusion: it does not want to let you go. The illusion doesn't want to let you go Home. It is meant to keep you here lifetime after lifetime after lifetime. That is the job of the illusion. So you have to work doubly hard to let go of all of your illusions, of all your judgments, and of your preferences.

You need to pray: "Please, Lord, strip away my being of illusion; strip it away!" And you need to stay intense with your desire. You can't go to sleep on yourself. You need to wake up and stay awake to your journey. Stay awake so you do not forget that you are not who you think you are. If you can understand this, then you will not fight and resist so

Notes: You need to pray; "Please, Lord, strip away my being of illusion; strip it away. In Absel desire / Stay awake

much the letting go of the various things that you need to let go of, the various illusions, because you will see them for the illusions that they really are.

You are not who you think you are at all. When you leave this body, you will remember nothing. You will take nothing with you, you will remember nothing, and your spirit will return Home. And if you take birth again, that is a different situation. If you take birth again, you carry the illusions with you to the next lifetime and have new illusions – more illusions – or find your way out of the illusion.

I would like you to meditate on the fact that you are not anything that you think you are; and when you die, no part of what you can think of now is going with you.

I will tell you a little funny story. The Lady and I were in some kind of competition in our transformations. There was a jealousy going on with The Lady and myself, and it had to do with God and if God had some favorite person among us. I was thinking that The Lady was that favorite person, and The Lady was thinking that I was God's favorite person. We were even projecting it into the true realm: "Who is the one that is with God in the true realm?" We were thinking, "We are going out there in the true realm, and Gourasana is going to be there, and all these different people are going to be there, and He is going to have this person and that person ..." It's not like that, because you

Notes:

10

let go of everything that you are. It is so funny to think back about that story – because you take nothing with you.

At the time of death, you need to be completely open to what is happening to you and what you are moving through. You can't have a concept of what it is going to look like on the other side. You will be with God to the degree that you have let go. You can't have any concept of how you think it is going to be with God, or what it is going to look like: if it is blue, if it is purple, if it is energy, if Gourasana is going to be there to greet you. You have no idea what is going to happen. You just have to be situated within yourself with Him and with no concepts. You have to give up everything to leave this plane.

Do not forget that what you are working on letting go of is your being of illusion. Otherwise, you are just doing the work and you are letting go, but then you are just creating another illusion after you let go; you are not letting go and then surrendering to God, which is what you have to do. We are not here to create a better being of illusion to become happier in this world. We are here to let go and find our way Home – no rebirth.

When you work on yourself, don't try to just make everything feel better inside, because then all you are doing is buying into your being of illusion that wants to feel better, that wants everything to be this way or that way. That is not the direction to go in. That is what I want you to understand from this talk: that you are not that being of illusion, the illusory self, the false self, the ego self. You are none of it. To work to defend your ego is ridiculous.

Try to hear and try to listen so you can really get it: *You are not who you think you are at all.* And when you go Home, you won't remember any of this lifetime at all.

Notes:

Personality

Spoken on July 28, 2007

Where does the personality fit into the teachings about breaking free of the ego, breaking the cycle of birth and death?

The personality is part of the being of illusion, and it's made up from the various incidents that have happened in your lifetime. Those incidents have molded you into becoming a certain way. Society also has had a big part in who you have become and what your personality is, in how your personality behaves. The defense mechanisms inside of you also have to do with how your personality is made up. For example, the protectiveness that you carry around has to do with your personality. The game that you play in the illusion has to do with how your personality is: meaning you have developed different ways of being, based on your particular illusions, based on how you function in the illusion, and based on how you want people to perceive you. This personality has to die along with everything else in your illusory being in order for you to break free. You have to let your personality go.

Notes:

You have to start to see the personality and how it talks and how it behaves with other people. If you start to look at it – look at how it talks and interacts with other people – you will just start to be quiet rather than have your personality engage itself. You will just say, "Thy will be done," and be quiet and prayerful. When you are around other people, don't talk, and just listen; absorb what is being said by other people. Talk if there is something that you need to say. But, if there is nothing you need to say, be quiet. If you do need to speak, then be deep when you speak, so that there is little chance of your personality engaging.

There is a type of slang-talking that people do that is all part of personality. Some people have a constant attitude, and that attitude is all personality. It is all illusion and it all needs to be given up. You need to drop it all. Pay attention and start to see what your personality is and what it does. You can simply make the decision, "I'm not going to do that anymore." There are so many deeper things that you have to work on to break free, so let go of all of these surface parts of your personality.

This talk is for people that want to break the cycle of birth and death. This particular talk is about breaking free. Those who are serious will hear the teaching I am talking about and will say, "Oh. I am going to start right away practicing not allowing my personality to take over."

Notes: Pray for awareness
"Thy will be done"
If you speak be deep

You have to control the ego. You can't be one big ego running around. You have to have control when you are going through the annihilation of the false self. With your true part, you have to be in control of what you are doing.

If you want to break free and you don't do this, it is just because of your resistance. Because you *can* do this part. You might not want to do it, but you might as well get on with it. This is a battle that isn't even a battle. It's just a letting go. It's just awareness. You may not know how to be or what to do, and that is why I give you the example of talking less and just being silent and responding only if you are spoken to. It will take some humility to do this. Just respond to questions without a big personality. Just talk normally without any big personality around it.

Your friends can help you to see your personality if you will let them. That is why it is important to have association with others who are also on the path when you are on the path endeavoring to break free. You need the help of others. (Of course, some people can just take my guidance and just live by themselves, and they are so serious that they just take my guidance and they understand it and they do it.)

If you think your true self is going to have your personality, you are wrong. Your personality has got to go, so start to practice letting it go right now. It is part of the being

Notes:

of illusion and it must go. Don't hang on to it. It may be a little strange for a while to learn how to be without your personality traits. That is why you need to be a little quiet. Don't speak. Don't engage in idle chatter; that will help you.

Don't take years to do this; just do it. Just start moving with it. Move with everything that I say and you will just never stop moving. You just keep moving and moving and moving. If you take all of my guidance and put it all together, you will just be moving and letting go and moving and letting go: closer and closer to God and freer and freer. Ultimate freedom is waiting; it is not a pipe dream. But you don't have any time to waste. You truly don't have any time to waste. You must wake up and start to run toward the light. Whatever it is that you need to do to let go, you have to do.

Good luck.

Notes:

Break the Habits of the Ego

Spoken on September 9, 2007

When you are working on letting go of parts of your ego, one thing you need to remember is that the ego that needs to be dismantled and let go of is not you. You think that it is you, but it is not you. It is what makes up the being of illusion. *It is not you.*

It is not something to lie on the floor and cry about. It is something to discover, something to see, and it is something to become sick of. This is something to realize. Remember, this is a path of self realization. So you want to realize that "The ego is not anything of myself. It is not serving me for coming into the pure love of God; that's for sure!"

When you sit back and you look at the ego, you can see it; you can see how it acts and how it makes you behave. Whether it makes you behave in a good way or a bad way, it all has to go. And if you are someone who wants to go to God, you are going to discover and realize very fast what this ego is.

Notes:

Then, when you see it, you let go of it. Have enough control in your being and in your mind that when you see it, you say, "I don't want that anymore. That is serving no one. It's just going to hold me back on my path to self-discovery." You do this because you can see, "There isn't any part of my self in that. That is just something that attached itself to me and became a part of me at some point, and I don't want it anymore. Good-bye."

The habits of the ego are things that you need *to control* so that they are not going to be living as a part of you anymore. You begin to watch what you say, watch how you behave, and watch how you are. Don't just be your being of illusion. No! Develop control over what you say, how you speak, and who you associate with.

If you are just going to associate with people that want to live in their being of illusion, that is going to drag out your being of illusion. You are going to be in your being of illusion when you are with them. That is why people who are transforming tend to not associate with old friends that are just hanging out in their being of illusion, because when your true being starts to come out, it is very uncomfortable to be around people that are just hanging out in the illusion. If you are around people who are engaged in some truth or some dancing where there is some real connection, that is another story. But it is not a good thing to hang around with

Notes:
_____

_____

_____

people where you let your illusion come up completely, and there is no room for your true being that is coming forth to be the way that it is.

Once you say, "This ego part that I have discovered is going to be dead now. I'm not going to let it live anymore," then the subconscious will get the message that "This part is not going to exist in me anymore. It has nothing to do with God. It is not serving me in any way, and now I'm going to let it go completely. I don't know how I'm going to be without it, but I'm not going to be with it." You must do that time after time after time, every time you see, "Oh, my ego talks and behaves like this. No. No more."

You are going to change, and you are going to find out that there is not a whole lot of personality in you. Maybe there is not a whole lot of joking around in you anymore as you are changing out of your being of illusion. Maybe there is going to be some quiet and some depth. Maybe you are going to find that the personality that you have been carrying around needs to be cleaned up until there is the personality that is compatible with who you are becoming, and then *that* will fall away as more of your true being takes over.

But you have to do this now. This is not such a hard thing. You just start letting go.

Don't be ashamed. Everyone is filled with the ego self. While you are working on yourself, you may need to

Notes:

do some crying, because finally you are letting go. But in letting go of the habits of the ego, it is more about awareness than release of emotions. The habits are things that are with you every single day. Be constantly looking for them and letting go of them. You pick up the spoon and then it is time to let go, so you put the spoon down; that is how fast the letting go is. You just have to start to see it and realize, "Aha, got you there." And then – no more; you let go. This is for someone that wants to break freer and freer and for someone that wants to go Home. It is very serious that you do that work very, very fast: just one thing after the other, after the other, after the other – let go.

You can see your own ego. You don't even need to be with others to see it. But by being with others, then there can be some help for you if you can't see your ego personality.

Then there are parts of your ego that you are desperately hiding and you don't want anyone to know about. But *why* are you doing that? Why? If you want to be free, then why are you hiding? *This has to change.* I can take you Home, but *you have to do your part.* It has got to be fast on your part. You have to just say, "Yes, I am ready, I am stalwart, and I will go fast. If there is some way to go faster, then I am going to be one of the ones that are going to go very, very, very fast. I will let go." And it doesn't matter how much it hurts to let go.

Notes:

Usually, spiritual masters do not even break one person free. But this is the most powerful Incarnation, and with the Host and with the guidance that is coming in, you can make it very, very quickly. But you have to be willing to let go. Let go, let go, let go, let go, let go, let go, let go, let go.

Thank you.

Notes:

About the Ego

Spoken on August 12, 2007

Spiritual transformation is about letting go of the ego. Everything that you think you are, everything that you think you will be, every way that you have put yourself together, every way you hold yourself, everything you think, every way you walk, every way you talk, every way you smile, the way you eat, is all ego. The things about you that you think are nice, the things you think are good qualities that you have learned or that were passed on to you or that you saw somewhere and so you adopted them and everyone in the world thinks you are so great, that you are the sweetest guy in the world – *these things are all ego.*

It is like the microfiber that makes up your whole being is all illusion. Until you are completely naked of ego, everything about your self is illusion. *Nothing in you, whatsoever at all, has any reality.* It is all going to be gone. When you are taking your last lifetime and you are working toward complete freedom, you will not make it back to the Source unless it is all gone – except that which is necessary to keep the body able to function and talk. That part of the ego stays so that you can do what you are doing to function

Notes:

in a body. But every other single thing, you have to completely drop and let go of.

You should be working on your ego *by yourself.* You shouldn't wait until someone tells you, "That's your ego." But when someone tells you something about your ego, don't feel bad about it. That is the wrong way to look at it. You want the help so that you *can* break free. You shouldn't feel bad when someone is pointing out your ego. In fact, *you should want to know about your ego.* You should want to know what your ego is. You should want someone to sit down and tell you what they see about your ego, so it can help you, so you can see more, and so you can get to work on letting it go. Because it is no easy thing to let go.

It is not an easy thing to completely let go of the whole being of illusion, the whole ego structure. That is why there is special assistance here to help. The special assistance is here in order to help everybody to let go of the ego. But people on the Path are not hammering away at the ego like they need to.

People are hanging on and resisting what they need to go through. If you are hanging on to every little thing that you have to let go of, you are just going to drown. You want to get your connection with God in your heart very strong, and then you want to go shoot your arrow toward Him. And if you don't want to call it God, go to the Source. Just connect

Notes:

to God and keep your arrow pointed to Him. Don't go into wallowing. Don't go down feeling bad about yourself. Don't waste your time going into negative things. Just go to Him.

I know it is really hard to see and accept all these things about your ego, but you want to hurry up, because there is so much deep inner stuff that you have no clue about that you have to let go of. You are not anything that you think you are. You are not any part of your mind. Your mind is going to completely change. Everything is going to completely change inside of you.

If you are not sure what to let go of, look at your ego. For example, look at how you walk. Just slow down and take a look at how you walk. See what kind of attitude you have when you walk. It started with David Swanson.* I was looking at him; he had this bouncy walk that he used to do. And Gourasana wanted into that body, and Gourasana was not going to bounce around like that. So David had to stop that completely. So just slow down and take a look at how you walk. See what kind of attitude you have when you walk.

Work on yourself. Don't wait to get help from a spiritual leader. Don't wait to be in a workshop. Work on yourself every day. That is why I gave you so many teachings. Look for your ego and make a plan: "This part of my ego is getting

---

* David Swanson is the man who gave his life so that Lord Gourasana could manifest in this world.

Notes:

_____

_____

cut out right now, because I'm not going to let it live. I'm going to basically choke it to death."

If focusing on breaking free is a distraction, then forget it. Don't even focus on that. If you are trying to get some state of enlightenment, forget about it, because it is not going to be what you think it is.

When you are enlightened, there is still suffering in the body and the mind. When you are enlightened, you don't just sit there without any problems. Of course, you are free of a lot of things. And you are detached from as much as you want to be detached from. If you want to be detached from everything and sit in a cave, you can. If you want to come out and be with people and help people, you can. Whatever you want to do, you can. That is the ability of an enlightened one.

If you don't work on the being of illusion every day, attaining enlightenment is going to take a very, very long time.

Are there any questions?

Disciple 1: Kalindi, is it the ego, itself, that prevents me from working on myself at a level that you are speaking?

Kalindi: Yes. The ego doesn't want to die, because then that is the end of everything. The ego doesn't want to die. That's why it's so hard to break free of all illusion. If you have the desire to break free, then you need to pull together all of

Notes:

your desire, listen to my teachings, and work on yourself like crazy, because there is no time to waste. You are going to die before you know it. It is up to you to do the work. A spiritual master can only guide you. I am bringing in energy that will help you, and Gourasana is bringing in massive power to help.

It is not an easy thing to hear that every single thing, everything about you has to die for you to achieve ultimate freedom. You can keep on working on yourself forever and becoming a better person, working on this little piece and that little piece, but the path that I am offering to ultimate freedom is not that.

Gourasana told us in the very beginning that you are not that being of illusion and everything that you think you are has to go. It is in *Breaking the Cycle of Birth and Death**. I think people have read that so many times, but they have never stopped to think, "What does He mean?" He said that letting go of the ego is a very hard thing to do, and it is worse than death many times over. Death is an easy thing by comparison, because you are just changing bodies. We are used to doing that. It is just a normal thing. But to go all the way, to meet the Source and go into the Source *while you're alive is the hardest thing to do*. The only ego that you are going to be left with is what keeps the body on course,

---

* Gourasana, *Breaking the Cycle of Birth and Death*, Miracle of Love, 4th Edition, 2007.

Notes:

26

to be able to go to the bathroom, preach, to do whatever the body is supposed to do. The whole body is ego.

Disciple 2: When you are looking at the ego and you want to let it go, do you need to know specifically what it is? Like righteousness or arrogance? Or if you feel something, and you know it's ego, but you are not exactly sure what it is, do you have to know what it is, or can you just let it go?

Kalindi: You can just let it go.

Disciple 2: Pray to let that go, whatever it is.

Kalindi: No, not even pray, just do it! You don't have to pray for all these things. You know most of what your ego is. You see it and that's it: Let it go. Don't waste your time praying and praying. Remember: God helps those that help themselves. So help yourself and do the work that *you* need to do. Praying for these things to go away is wasting time. It's procrastination.

If it is a big thing that you have to let go of, then you need to ask for some help. If you've done everything that you can do, then you need to pray for some help. But you can't just pray and pray and think it is going to go away. You have to let go.

When you let go of the bigger things, all the smaller things that were connected to the bigger things automatically go. So you want to work on the bigger things, not on the smaller things. If it is driving you crazy to work on the big-

Notes:

ger things, then work on something else that you can work on and leave that big one alone until later when it is more accurate to work on it.

You have to keep moving and keep letting go of something *every single day:* You have to keep letting go of the next thing and the next thing and the next thing. Just keep letting go of one thing after the next, and don't get stuck, because you want to keep moving. You don't need to think about it so much; it is all going to come up, and when it does, let it go.

Disciple 3: How do you know when you have let something go and can move on to the next thing?

Kalindi: If you haven't let go of it, it will keep resurfacing; move with what is happening, and then you will feel it. You can feel everything that is going on inside of you. You can. And when you are willing to see it all and own it all as false, then you can let go: "Well, this is what my ego is made of, and it all has to go." If you haven't let go of something, it will come back up and it will stop you. It will get in your way repeatedly. It will be the one thing that keeps coming back up, or the two things that keep coming back up. Those are the things that you just have to keep going after. At a certain point you are going to have to get on the floor and just cry and cry and cry. But at that point, you will be connected to God. The last parts will go, because either you will see them or if you don't, other people will. They will keep resurfacing.

Notes: *Every single day you have to let go of something*

Don't take the attitude that anything is gone. You have to be very humble on a spiritual path. Someone traveling a path like this is very humble. The part of you that comes out and is not humble *is all ego.* Just have the attitude of "I don't have any right at all to say anything about anyone, and there is no one that I am better than. No one." Humility. Humility is the first thing you have to get. Get humility, not false humility that people do on spiritual paths.

Do not have any false worship going on. I, as your spiritual master, don't want any of that. I am only here to help you understand how to do the transformational work and to help you connect to God. That is all. And I am here to bring you guidance. There cannot be any worship going on – none. Give your worship to the one that it belongs to, and that is the Lord, God. He doesn't even want any worship. But when you have those kinds of feelings, write a letter to Him or put some flowers on an altar. I am not here to be worshiped.

What gives me the most pleasure is that you are doing the spiritual work and that you are making it Home. That is all. You are doing it and you are making it. When I talk about false humility, please try to hear what I am saying. Humility is not something where you walk around with your head hanging down, and you become worthless, and you don't feel like you should say anything to anyone,

Notes:

because you feel you don't know anything. That is not what I am talking about. Humility is one of the most real feelings inside your heart that you have with God. It is not some fake thing that makes you look like a weird person in the world. I don't want people to turn humility into something weird, when in fact it is a holy thing; it is a very Godly thing.

Are there any questions?

Disciple 3: I'm wondering how much you need to know about your ego, and how much you need to know all of its tricks and all what the ego does, in order to let go of it? Do you really need to very clearly see how the ego works and exactly what it does in order to let it go? Or can you just feel it and know it's there and let it go from that place of feeling it? If you don't really know what it is, can you already let it go at that level?

Kalindi: You have to know.

It *is* the illusion and the illusion, remember, does not want to go. You have to see it, and you have to get to know the way it works. If you cut it off over here, it's going to come up over there. You have to shut all of the doors. You have to get to know it and shut every door where it is coming in. You have to see where it is going on: "It's going on over there, now over here, and now it's trying to come out over here." There are some things you can just let go

Notes:

of, but you need to identify the big ways that it works. You need to get to know the illusion and how it is working in you so you can dismantle it.

Disciple 4: One way that I see my ego is, it feels like I'm sitting in front of a wall. And the only way to get around the wall is to trick it. I believe in that wall. And I don't know how to bypass it permanently. So far I've managed to get past it, but it's coming back. It's like I let it go, but then it comes back.

Kalindi: That is because the way you do your spiritual work most of the time is just in workshops; you do a workshop, and then the next workshop, and then the next seminar. But you don't meditate every night. Part of my guidance is that you need to meditate every night for one hour. You have to go deep. You can't just do this type of spiritual work without meditation. *You have to meditate* and go deeper into the real connection inside of you. It's that real connection inside of you that is going to fortify you and bring you closer to truth, more and more truth. You will come to more and more truth as you do this battle with the ego. But if you do not connect and strengthen your connection within to the Source, to God, and take God's help and take the energy that God's bringing in to help you, there is no way. If you are not going to meditate and strengthen your connection like this, I would say, don't do this work to break free. Instead, go on the freer

Notes:

and freer path that we have created. Don't do the advanced ego work. Don't try to break free. You will have a miserable life. The people that are doing the break-free work are getting their rewards; they are going deeper and they are getting freer – it is working. But if you don't follow my guidance, then you're going to have problems. If you don't meditate, there's no way to do this work, because you have to connect, and that connection has to become greater and greater and greater as the illusion becomes less and less and less. Because what is going to fill you if you don't meditate? You are counting on your illusion to replace your illusion. So your illusion is tricking itself back and forth, and there is no God in there. There is no spirit Source that is feeding you. And you need to meditate to have that.

If you don't meditate for an hour every night, I say you are not as serious as you need to be. We have the meditations at the Center, and that is for a certain kind of meditation, for mass movement of a group together, but that is not enough meditation. You have your half an hour morning meditation to do your RE's* and prepare to come into the day. Then at night you have an hour where you should meditate. And if you need to meditate today, don't wait until the night when meditation is happening at the

---

* Kalindi's guidance is to meditate in the morning and take time to write down, in order to keep a calm and empty mind, things that come to you that you need to remember, which she terms "RE's."

Notes:

Center. When everything is building up inside of you and you need to meditate, meditate that day *as soon as you can.*

Spiritual laziness is a very hard habit to break. A lot of people have this. They are spiritually lazy. But they found a great Mission where there's a lot of love and there's a lot of God. And they want to get freer. There are a lot of things going on, but for the ones that want to break free, they've become spiritually lazy, which is a very *hard* habit to break. If that's how you've begun your spiritual life, and you've been going for eight years, it's very hard to break that. But maybe now the desire is going to open up in you. But it's totally up to you what you want to do.

Remember, Gourasana said that you can go ten years with seemingly no results, and then after the tenth year results start to come. You have to also understand that this is the hardest spiritual work to do, what we are endeavoring to do. That is why you need a spiritual master to do this. I am saying, "Listen to your master and follow the guidance. If you don't meditate, how are you going to make it?"

If people listen to the guidance, their transformations will speed up. Listen to my talks.

Everybody is trying to go to the seminar so they can heal their being of illusion. Isn't that a crazy thing, that people are going through a whole process of trying to heal the being of illusion? Everybody comes back and feels so good after they have gone through another layer of healing the being of illusion, and now it feels better. What about surrender? And what about getting on the floor three nights a week and screaming "Almighty Lord?!" What about just doing it and taking Gourasana's help and just moving with Him? What about taking The Lady's example, what she did? She never did a workshop. She was on that ground for eight hours a day for three years crying and screaming or trying to get through the wall. Just hammering the wall down. And the only one thing she ever worked on was when Gourasana told her, "Find out where your anger came from," because she had massive anger. The only thing she ever worked on was that massive anger, and she did it all on the floor. She worked on that massive anger, and she worked on her full and absolute surrender.

Surrender to God and let the energy of Him take you over, and just gut it out on the floor with Him. Just the light versus the dark; the light versus the illusion. That is possible. That is the fastest way. But you have to have *so much desire and so much love for God and so much love for humankind.* It is possible to do it that way.

Just decide; go for it. Let's go. Don't feel bad that you have an ego, because all you do have is an ego that has to be worked on, and as it dies, more love will fill you. Because love and light is who you really are.

Notes:

Good or Bad –
It Is All Illusion

Spoken on August 15, 2007

I want to say a few words regarding your day-to-day life and working on letting go of your ego, your being of illusion, who you think you are.

Everything you do all day long should be a letting go, because you will see your ego all day long. You will see how it works. You will see what it does. You will come to know all the various ways that your ego structure is set up. Once you see it, you can start to let go of it.

I am sure your housemates – if you live with others – are happy to point things out to you. It is not such an easy thing to do to point things out to each other. If your house-mates or friends or family point something out to you about how your ego is behaving, you should have nothing but humility and say, "Thank you very much." Then you should go after working on that part of the ego and letting it go. It could be a good part of your ego; it could be a bad part of your ego. It doesn't matter. Good or bad, it is all illusion.

You should want people to say something to you

Notes:

about your ego, so you can see it and let it go. It will get to the point where nobody really needs to say anything to you anymore, because you are on that floor in meditation working on yourself. You are meditating and you are working on yourself and you are letting go so much, all the time.

You don't have to figure out if someone is telling you the truth or not or if you believe it or not, because practically speaking, it is all ego anyway. You just need to say, "Thank you very much," and then go about your business and take a look at what they said, and say, "Hmm, that part of my ego has to go, too." Everyone who is working on themselves should be happy to be helping each other, and everyone should be happy to be on such a path to freedom.

Look at The Lady as an example. The Lady took a very, very, very fast path. It was a very hard path. I say it was so hard, because what she did on her path was so intense. She asked for the pot of gold at the end of the rainbow and nothing less than the pot of gold, and she wouldn't pick her head up to look at anything else until she found that gold. She was hard on herself; she was hard on herself and hard on her own illusions. She could see them all, she worked on them all, and she didn't let up. Then at a certain point, she could see enough light that she would start to let the light in.

I want The Lady's path to be an example for everyone. You can really get going. Every one of you will be with the Host. The Host is plentiful. Your true self is in that Host. You don't have to believe that; nevertheless, that Host is here with the energy to take you Home, with the assistance to take you Home.

Understand that everyone is full of ego. As fast as possible, dump everything that you can in the trash. You don't have to hang on to all of the stuff of the ego. You can just throw things out and just change, change, change, change. *Change is good.* Keep changing. Change what you wear. Change your house around. Change your bed around. Keep changing things, because that makes you change inside. It makes things change inside of you; the whole illusion gets stirred up inside of you; and that is when you can let go of things.

I am going to say this one time and I hope that you hear it: *Don't leave your path. Don't stop.* If you do, chances are you won't come back, because the path is so difficult. You won't want to start up again. If you are fortunate enough to have found the path and you are moving along on the path, whether it is to break free or to get freer and freer, keep going! Keep going, because you are breaking freer and freer every single day, and you are getting closer and closer to the endless love of God every single day. How fast you move forward is based on your desire. You can always move forward faster and you can always slow down, *but never, ever give up.*

Good luck. I love you.

Notes:
_____

_____

_____

Want the Help

Spoken on August 13, 2007

One of the most important things that you can do to help yourself during your transformation is to receive help, to reach out and allow someone else to help you spiritually.

If someone comes forward to help you, you need to be in enough humility to hear what that person has to say. They have taken the necessary steps to come toward you to tell you something that they think will be valuable for you, *so take the position of humility.* Don't put your ego forward and have the attitude of "What do you know about me, and what are you talking about?" Be humble and just listen to what they have to say, because they may have something very important to say to you that is a key ingredient to unwinding your whole ego.

You should immediately be humble and completely listen to anyone who has something to say to you, and get what it is that they are trying to say. Help can come from anywhere; it doesn't have to only be someone on a spiritual path that can help you. It could be someone you meet on the street. Want to receive spiritual help when help is coming toward you.

Notes:
_____

_____

_____

Search for others that you know who are perhaps more advanced on the path than you, or who you know can see areas of your ego better than you. Do this because you are so sincere and you want to break free as soon as possible of this horrendous ego that you are dragging around.

Seek the association of others who have gone before you in transformation. Ask them if they will kindly talk to you, or come over to your house, perhaps have dinner with you, or take them out for dinner and ask them, "Can you please help me to see my ego and what it is doing? Because I don't see it clearly and I want to be rid of this atrocity of darkness. Can you please help me? I don't know what to do to get rid of it. Even if I saw it, I don't know what I would do. Can you please help me?"

Want the help of others. Living in a house with others is so valuable because you can sit in your living room together and talk to each other and help each other to see the different ways that the ego is working. You have each other right in the house. You can have a "seminar" every single night and help each other to see the ego.

A very important spiritual teaching of mine is to help one another spiritually. Don't feel like you are better than everyone else so that you shouldn't have to do this type of work. Everybody needs to do this type of work.

Notes:

_____

_____

How are you going to make it to God otherwise? Help each other and accept the help.

The ego has to be exposed and it has to be let go of. Some of the egos are very strong-willed and do not want to let go, so people have to keep pointing out to that person over and over and over: "There's your ego again; there's your ego again; there's your ego again." People with an ego like that don't like to hear it. They don't like to hear it, so they start to become angry. When someone points out your ego, you should say, "Thank you very much for taking the time to talk to me about my illusion, about my ego, so I can work on it now. Do you have any further suggestions of how I can work on this and what I can do to get rid of it?"

Be loving to one another. When the ego comes up in each other, you have to remember that that ego is not who that person is. That person is the loving light of God. All of the illusion that you see in them is false; it is not who that person is. You are just trying to help that loving soul to get free from all of the false ego. *Try to remember this all of the time.* Practice this all of the time: "This poor suffering being of light is trapped underneath this horrendous ego. I'm going to keep helping this person so they can get free of it, because I know they are only suffering in there. And no matter what comes out of their mouth and no

Notes:

40

matter how nasty they might be, it is not them. They are only love underneath all that." Help one another. We are in a big battle and we are in it all together.

Notes:
_____

_____

_____

Transcendence

Spoken on July 11, 2007

Transcendence is a word that I haven't used before, because the word itself can possibly lead people to go into different states of denial in areas that actually need to be felt and released. But there is a way to travel this path to freedom transcending illusions in order to let them go. For some people, that is the most natural way to go.

Transcending something is when something comes up that is illusory or that needs to be let go of, and you are able to see it with your awareness and say, "Aha, okay, now here is an illusion. Here is something that I need to let go of in order to move forward." It may have a feeling to it or it may not. If it doesn't have any feeling to it, it is very easy for someone who is a transcendentalist to just see it thoroughly and then let it go, *really* just let it go and continue the path.

You need to know where it's *necessary* to transcend something. It means that you are going to have a feeling inside of you that you are going to be unresolved about, and you are going to let go and transcend it and be okay. Now, I don't want you to take this as some kind of an excuse to not

Notes:

42

feel deeply what it is that you need to feel and face. But you are going to have to just let go and transcend many things within, and many things that happened to you in your life. It's just like "Too bad, there is no time to deal with this, and I can't feel it and I can't move through it. I'm just going to let go and transcend it." Just let go. Rise above it and let it go. That doesn't mean you won't still have the feeling of it inside. But slowly that feeling will melt away.

There are times on the path when there is some pain to feel or some sacrifice to deal with and then to transcend whatever is in the way. In those cases, use awareness to take a look at the situation. But there cannot be repression going on in any way. Maybe you have to release your emotions for five or twenty minutes or go into meditation two times. Then you have the knowing: "Well, I have to give this up anyway and I don't want to waste any time, so let me feel it to the depth where it needs to be felt, and then after tonight I will release it and get on with things."

That is how you travel this path in a transcendental way. You just move and let go, move and let go, move and let go. You don't hang on to anything. You release to the depth that you need to release to and then you move on, because there are so many things that need to be faced. You just move on and move on and move on and move on, as you are going deeper and deeper. Because there is no repression, you are allowing yourself to feel what needs to be felt, but then you are releasing it and just moving on.

That is the best way to approach a rapid spiritual path. It is not easy, but for those of you that have the type of makeup that can transcend illusion, then I suggest that you do that, calling upon the Lord and letting go just like that. When it comes time to let go, you know, "Okay, it is time to let go," and then you *really* let go, because otherwise it will catch up with you later. You have to let go *at* the time.

Really, the best way to walk the path is to transcend the things you can. Just go above them. Just forget them. What is it worth hanging on to all of these things? God is waiting for you. Just go! Don't hang on to things. Just let go. Then if you need to cry, cry a little bit and then finish with it and then let go, but *let go*. This body had to transcend everything, because there just simply wasn't time to go through a path of crying and crying and crying. That was because this body was manifesting as a spiritual master right away, and it didn't have any time to go through anything and was already taking everybody on spiritually. So that path is possible for you. I pray for all of you, that if possible, you can travel your path that way.

Notes:

Letting Go
Is the Way to God

Spoken on August 15, 2007

One thing that I would like everyone to understand about awakening, about enlightenment, about going Home, is that your entire ego structure – your being of illusion down to the last grain within you, even your mind and your psyche – *is not you*. Not anything that you know to be you, not anything that you think – not anything – is you.

Just the little spirit soul inside of you that came into this world is you. And that is the part that will return. Everything else is just dust; it is dust in the wind. Your entire makeup and personality, everything – none of it's you, and that is what has got to die. It has got to be annihilated – completely.

That is the work that you have to do, and you have to get on the floor to meditate. You have to cry and you have to beg and you have to scream from your guts. You have to scream from your heart to God to help you to make it in this lifetime and not resist the battle that has to be fought for your soul. It is hard enough, without resisting.

Notes:
_____

_____

The hardest thing to do on this earth is to become enlightened. There are spiritual masters here in the Mission, and the Heavenly Host is here on this earth, the Lord is here, and there is so much special assistance available now. That is why you can make it if you want to, but you have to work very hard for many, many years to make it Home.

One thing that I want to share with you is that as long as you have a body, you will have some ego. I don't know if this has been thoroughly understood in this world. As long as you have a body, there will always be some personality connected to your body. Whether it is a personality that sits and meditates in a cave, or whether you have a mission to do for God that requires you to walk around and wear clothes, you have a personality. Whatever the case may be, if you have a body and it talks and walks, then it has a personality. That ego won't drop off of you until your body drops from this world. Your body is the last part of the ego that will fall away.

You will be working on letting go and letting go and letting go all the way until you leave this world. There will be no time that you won't be letting go. But you will learn that there is always ecstasy and love on the other side of letting go. Letting go is the way to God, and it produces love and ecstasy every time.

Notes:

_____

_____

_____

The more you let go of the illusory being, the more space there is for the presence of God in your being. When more of who you really are connects to God, the more space there is for God in your being. The more you let go of the illusory being, the more you can connect to what is real.

You have to start dropping chunks of the illusory being, and your illusion doesn't want that; your ego doesn't want that. So you can't spend so much time playing around and trying to figure everything out with your mind. You have to just do the work *the way that I am guiding you to do it.* If you are doing it a different way and playing around in the illusion and not being deep, then you are going to find yourself being caught by the illusion, time after time after time.

Notes:

SURRENDER TO MEDITATING

*The Only
Solution
to the Problem
Is to
Go Deep.*

GOURASANA

Go into Meditation Connected to God

(A guided, "directed" meditation*)

Spoken on June 4, 2008

This is a directed meditation, which means that it is necessary for you to follow each direction that I speak as you are meditating.

Get yourselves comfortable sitting in an upright position. If you need to sit against a wall or in a chair to help you to sit up, that is okay. But it is necessary that you sit up. If you have some type of illness that requires you to lie down, then that is also okay. But in general, you should always begin your meditation sitting up.

Now close your eyes and begin to go within.

Find a deeper place than the surface place that you live in during the day. Find a depth. In a sense, this depth is a physical feeling within your body; the feeling starts at the middle portion of your body, inside, and runs from your chest area all the way down, until you get to the bottom of where that depth can go. It is not just deep in your heart.

---

* Available in audio form, from www.miracle.org., so you can use it to meditate with.

Notes:

50

It is deep in your being, which includes everything: your heart, your soul, your longing. This depth is inclusive of everything, and I want you to simply begin to go within, into that depth.

On the way to that depth, you may have to pass through and deal with some certain blocks to get to that depth. There may be some different blocks that are stopping you from getting to the bottom of that depth, like feelings – agitation or fear. You may need to release emotions, to scream or cry to get these things out of the way. That is where I want you to go now, very deep.

I think a lot of people who have been using the Modern-Day Meditation may have been meditating with a concept that they have to meditate by going into all of the feelings, like all of the agitation or fear, until they finally get to a connection. And they think that getting connected is what meditation is. They think that the connection that they finally get to is the last thing in their meditation. The truth is that you need to go through these different blocks and feelings and get deep as fast as you can and get connected, *so that you can be with God to begin your meditation.*

The first part of what you *were* calling "meditation" you can call "pre-meditation." It is like emptying out. It is going within, emptying out, and traveling toward your connection.

Notes:
_____

_____

_____

Just keep going and keep focusing on going deeper, deeper, deeper. You are going on a quest for the deepest connection that you can find where you know you are connected. If you want to call that connection "God," you can call it God. You can simply just call it "connected." Once you get to that place, where you are connected, all of these other surface things will be gone; because to become connected, you will have released all of the different things that were blocking that connection. (Sometimes people can simply just get connected and go deep right away.) Once you reach that connection and are in that connection, *then* you can move forward into the actual meditation of going within.

Meditation, by definition, produces union: union with God, union with the Divine, union with All That Is. It's union. You need to begin your meditation from your connection.

This is how you need to start every meditation, connected. Otherwise, you try to go within by doing what *your mind thinks* you should do. But if you will do it the way I am directing you, then you can be sure that you are going into meditation connected – in union, together, focused on and connected to God, in whatever way you want to call God.

When you are connected, situate yourself in that connection and enter your meditation from there. You can visualize sitting like the Buddha, deep with God with your connection. You will not be taking any baggage into the

Notes:

meditation, other than yourself and your desire for union with the Divine.

From this connected place, begin your meditation without any concept of how it is going to be. Just stay deep. Be with God and go deeper and deeper. Perhaps you will be moved to tears. Perhaps you will encounter the transformational energy. Perhaps you will be calm. And go deeply into all of these experiences you are having.

Each experience will be brand new every time you meditate, because you are meditating in your connection, letting God guide you. You are not in this other place of working on all of these blocks and feelings; you are meditating. He is taking you where He wants to take you. It is union with Him that is happening in your meditation. There is never a point where you are not with Him, because you got connected before you even started meditating.

You then just move in and out of different experiences while you are meditating with your prayer, "Please Lord, take me deeper. I want to be with You all of the time." You are meditating with whatever your prayer is, whatever you are asking. Then all of a sudden your meditation is just open, just universally open to anything and everything, to wherever and however God wants to move you. You are not thinking that you have to work through something or work on something.

Notes:

_____

_____

_____

And if you have any kind of problem, then you can take that into meditation – knowing specifically what the problem is – and you can ask, "What should I do about this problem?" If you need to cry about it, then you will cry about it. And if you are moving and moving and moving and all of a sudden you run into a block, then you will have to do what you have to do to go through that block. Perhaps you are just simply calm and just going deeper and deeper and deeper into the most incredible experience of calm. So many things are waiting for you in your meditation.

Then you let go and you start to move in a very open, free-flowing way. You just move. Very sensitive, you just start moving, you just go. Whatever comes up in your meditation, just move with it. Whatever comes up, that is what comes up; then *that* is what you have to move with. You will just be moved into the next thing, and then into the next thing, and into the next thing. You won't be trying to make something happen or trying to figure something out. You won't be asking, "Oh, what should I do, what direction should I go in?" like that, because God will be guiding you. He won't be telling you "Do this, do this," He will just take you and move you.

I think that is something many people are waiting to experience in meditation, and this is how it can happen.

So now just fall into your meditation and just go.

Notes:
_____

_____

_____

How to Pray

Spoken* by Gourasana on February 20, 1995

In the following passage, Gourasana is teaching people how to win the battles of the flesh and the spirit and to go through the dark nights of the soul by learning how to pray. His teaching is not just for the people that want to break the cycle of birth and death. The whole world is transforming and people are coming up against some very hard things, so everyone can benefit by Gourasana's teaching on how to pray.

Gourasana teaches how to succeed in battles with the illusion. The only way to win these battles is to meditate, to go very deep in meditation. If you find yourself covered over by illusion, He is teaching that you need to stay on the floor in meditation until your charge and your feelings about the matter that you're dealing with is gone, is diffused. He is teaching you to not get up in the middle of your meditation until you are connected. Once you are connected, you can return to a calm state and make intelligent decisions about what you need to do in your life, whether it be what God is asking of you or what

---

* Gourasana speaking How to Pray is available at www.miracle.org. It is very useful to have the audio version to listen to and meditate with.

Notes:

you need to do in your life. It's not that God can do it for you,
but you can approach Him to find answers.

This is a very important prayer to be learned, not in
its words, but in its intent and in its mood. Learn from an
Incarnation of God teaching us how to pray, how we must pray
to defeat the illusion to get out of this illusory world.

You have come to a very serious moment in your
life. More than in your life: in your very existence. The battle
that you now will fight with the darkness will make the
difference – or could make the difference – between getting
free from the material world, where you have been for
billions of years, or staying.

So when you find yourself having a hard time, I
suggest that, every time, you get down on your knees. Don't
lie flat out on the floor; don't do the one that you have
learned. Just get down on your knees and hands, and pray
with all the sincerity and with all the seriousness that the
moment calls for. You pray so sincerely to God to give you
the strength to win this battle with the illusion.

It's just going to be one battle after another, and you
can win every battle that you are going to be faced with.
And it is important to have the trust and faith in Me to
believe that that is true. There is no battle that you will be
in with the darkness that you cannot win.

Notes:

For instance, if you are on the floor, and you are praying so sincerely that you are giving it everything that you can, and still you feel like you're losing, then you begin to *beg to God*. You *beg* that:

> My dear Lord, I want nothing else but You. I am willing to do anything to once again go Home and be in Your arms. I will go through anything that I have to, to win the battles that I have to go through with the illusion. Please, give me the strength. Please, I am begging to You. I want nothing else. I am truly willing to do anything that You ask of me in order to re-establish the loving relationship that I once had with You. I will do anything. And while the things You may ask of me may be very, very difficult, I know – because of my sincerity – that You will help me and give me the strength to do every-thing that You ask of me. I know that You will help me succeed in this life because I care only for You.

Do you see? And you can just keep on praying until you are certain that you have put the illusion at bay, and you can stand up and be all right, and have won the battle.

When it comes down to it, your most immediate and most powerful weapon is prayer. It isn't in service; you can't get up and wash the dishes and have the pouring-in of energy that you need to fight the battle that is beginning.

Notes:

_____

_____

_____

There is nothing more powerful or more immediate that you can do than pray.

Pray out loud. That is the most powerful thing because that takes *more* humility. If you pray in silence, then you are like hiding a bit – it is less humble. But when you say it out loud so that people can hear you begging, showing your humility to everyone, because you care, you will do anything – praying out loud makes your prayers much stronger.

And you may just pray for a few seconds and suddenly find a rush of energy and strength, or you may need to pray for a long time, searching for the words, searching for different ways to ask for help, searching for different ways to address the Almighty, the Lord, the Father of Everything. But you don't get up from that floor until you feel that you are at least in equal strength with the illusion. It's not that precarious. Once you feel confident, you know you will be all right, then you can get up, and you will be perfectly safe.

Notes:

Pushing Down the Wall Into the Light

Spoken on August 22, 2006

This talk is for people who are just beginning this spiritual work and for everybody on the path. You don't have to be afraid anymore of whatever feeling or illusion that comes up within. You don't have to be resistant to it anymore. When the illusion comes up or when you are stuck or when a feeling comes up, *embrace it as good.* Don't get all freaked out about it. Just say, "Good, here it comes, here's the illusion, here's the darkness, now I'm stuck, good. Now I know what I have to do. I have to let go. That's all."

"I have to let go. It does not matter what the thing I have to let go of is. It does not matter what the feelings are that I am having. It doesn't matter what the feelings are about. It doesn't matter if I understand what is happening; I just know I have to let go now." And you get on the floor and you meditate. You push through that wall of illusion until you break it down, and again there is light and there is your connection to God. You push down the wall until

Notes:

you are again just moving forward with God, serving God, and moving forward again. Your consciousness is growing, everything is expanding and then ... "Whoop! Here it is again; here are all those feelings I don't like. There is that darkness. There are all those different blocks and feelings – shame and guilt and unworthiness and fear." You don't have to be afraid when a feeling or illusion comes up. All you have to do is say, "Uh oh, here it is again," and *get on the floor:* Get your scream towel, get your Kleenex and do your meditation work.

Push down the wall with Part One of the Modern-Day Meditation; release your emotions. Push forward into the light. Don't stay hung up in any idea of what you think you are crying about. It doesn't matter what you are crying about. What matters is that you break that wall down, push forward, and get back into the light. The issues don't matter. You can feel them for a few minutes, but just let them take you deeper into remembering, "I've got to push the wall down."

Don't forget you are going within in meditation to push the wall down. Whether it is tears or screaming or whatever it is you are feeling, do it with the intention of pushing down the wall so the light can come again. If you are meditating for any other purpose when you are up against a wall, then you are doing the wrong thing.

Notes:

When that wall comes and you feel separate, alone, unheard, like no one understands you, angry, or scared, or you feel hatred, it doesn't matter. When any of that comes up and you lose your connection, and all of a sudden you are in your mind and nothing is making any sense, it doesn't matter. All that matters is that you recognize, "Here's that pile of stuff again that keeps me separate from people, and from the love that I know that's inside of me. And I know I've tasted the love and the ecstasy of my connection with God many times. And there is nothing I want more than that. Even right now as I am swallowed up by this wall of darkness, there is a little part in me that knows the truth that I've found in my heart. And that little place gives me faith. It might get really covered over, and I can hardly feel my faith and my trust, but I feel it just barely enough to know that I have to push through this wall."

Your thinking has to be "Here it is, this big wall of stuff again," all the way through your transformation, until there are no more walls and you don't have to push through any more walls. In the advanced stages of transformation, you have the last walls that you have to push through as you walk the road Home into the Source, and there is very advanced work that you have to do.

In the beginning work and in the advanced work, your attitude has to be: "Here it comes again." Transfor-

Notes:

mation is all a process of breaking down the walls and letting the light get in to shine upon the next wall. It is all about you being open: "All right, let it come," and praying, "Lord, please free me."

The Lord shines the light in answer to your prayer. He shines the light on the part of you that is not in the light yet, the part of you that is covered by darkness. The Lord shines the light, and from your side, you are praying and pushing on whatever illusion is there. You are pushing through it, and you are pushing the illusion up into the light. The light is shining on the illusion, the darkness, and bam! – the light shines and the darkness hits the light. Then you just work on the side of the light, with your desire that is somewhere inside of you, even when you feel you are in darkness. Push your way through – push, push in meditation.

In your everyday life, use your awareness and try to understand what is happening when something comes up that you have to push through. It is in meditation that you push through. And be grateful that the light shined enough on something so that a wall has come up again. Know, "Okay, here we go. We are going into battle again. We will get through that wall, and on the other side there will be more light and more connection." This is the path of transformation that I am here to teach.

Notes:

Be happy when the wall hits, because that means the light of God is right there shining on it. It is like His hand is there helping you to get down on that floor and push through the wall. It's like you are giving birth to a new part of yourself and God is the doctor. You are giving birth and you have to push through. Then you will come through, and then a whole new being of light will be there – more consciousness and more awareness every time. You are in a process of labor, giving birth to your true self. And God is on the other side of all of it, and He is just shining light and just pulling for you, and helping you to give birth to yourself.

No more hiding in fear of your illusions coming up and how that feels. You want your illusion to come up; that is the transformation!

That is why we have meditations at the Centers and communities: so you can get on the floor and do your work. If you are at home and your illusion is coming up and you are not at a group meditation, get on your bed and work through it. That is why in the House Programs there is a meditation room in the house. Sound-proof your meditation room so you don't disturb the neighbors. Use your scream towels and meditate as the wall is coming up.

Have your meditation rooms set up at night so that if anybody needs to meditate, then they can go right in the meditation room at any time they need to. Be conscious in

Notes:

_____

_____

_____

your houses; know, "Wow, someone is in the meditation room letting go; maybe they need some help. I'm going to go in there and sit next to them." It is always helpful if someone is sitting next to you, supporting you while you are going through those walls. That's why it feels so safe in the meditation rooms at the Centers. So start to be aware in your house when someone is in the meditation room or when someone is letting go and going really deep: "Hey, maybe I'm going to go in there and meditate too." This is how you should be living as you are transforming.

I hope I have said it clearly enough so that the people just starting this work can understand what I mean by "wallowing" and "issues." When you just have one big clump of issues right in front of your face, and you can't get anywhere – when you can't get to your connection again because this thing is in front of you – get on the floor and move it. Then when it is cleared away and you can get up from meditating on the floor, you know you are okay and the illusion isn't in the way anymore, start to deal with your problem and figure out what actions to take.

With your awareness, start to deal with your problem of unworthiness. Don't deal with it being in it, but deal with it from having gone through the feelings around it, in meditation. Push the wall down until you are in a clear state and you are not feeling unworthy. Use your awareness

Notes:

to figure out what you can do about unworthiness, like thinking, "Well, maybe I can wear some clothes that help me not look unworthy." Start to make your list of actions that you can do about the situation. Do not sit around and wallow in it, "Poor me, poor me."

To figure out what to do about a problem, you are supposed to do the Modern-Day Meditation in a calm state. Get your intelligence going and figure out action plans for the problems that you have, because you can do something about each and every problem that you have going on inside of you that is keeping you from the light and love of God. That is what your awareness is supposed to be doing while you are in a calm state during meditation. You are supposed to be getting answers by asking, "What can I do about this problem? Because it's keeping me separate from God. I know I need to find the answers inside of myself, so I can take action, because I'm the one that needs to do it. I have to find what action I have to take to dislodge this thing; otherwise, the wall is going to keep coming back. I'm sick and tired of that wall coming down on top of me. I've got to save myself from this stuff that's going on inside of me. So these are my actions."

Do something about it. Release yourself. Don't hang on. You have got to let it go. What do you have to do to let it go? Do it! However many times you have to get on that floor, to crack the wall down, it doesn't matter. There will be more light every time.

There is more light and more information that will come to get you through whatever you need to go through in transformation. *But you have to be willing to let go.* Most people are on the floor crying about it, and begging God, "Please, please, please," but they are not doing their part to knock down that wall with their full desire: "Yes, I don't want this anymore. I don't want it!" They are lying there crying and they are praying to God, "I don't want it anymore; please take this," but they are not doing anything in their life to show God that they are doing their part of releasing it. God is just sitting there: "I'm doing everything I can do. I'm giving them all the light and all the love and all the information they need. They're not doing anything with it except to lie on the floor and wallow, "Poor me."

God has given the intelligence to every person to have the information they need to get out of their predicament. It is going to mean change, movement forward, and letting go. Just let it go, like a piece of trash. Walk away from it: "I don't want this. This isn't what I want. Bring that wall up; I'm going to hack it down. And I'm going to cry and scream." You hack it down and get up, and if it is still there, ask, "What am I going to do about it?" Then make an action plan. This explanation ties the whole Modern-Day

Notes:

Meditation together with how to use that meditation for the purpose of breaking down these walls of illusion.

Listen to the Gourasana *How to Pray* talk*: "Please, help me to knock these walls down. Help me, please. Please help me." That prayer will pull in the light of God and the special assistance of God that He's brought here to help you. It will pull that to you. It is a special assistance from God that will help you to break free fast. He will just shine awareness, and the energy will go into your body. All of the energy from God that is here to help you will just come pouring into you if you are calling for it and begging for it.

If you want God that badly, just be begging Gourasana, "Please, help me. I want this so badly." The special assistance is going to be pulled to you like a magnet. It is going to help you in ways beyond your mind, so that by the next day after you do that meditation, you will think, "I don't know what happened, but I don't have any of that stuff going on anymore." Illusions and feelings that would have taken you twenty years to work through, all of a sudden felt different when you got up in the morning. You were in bed the night before, and you prayed when you went to sleep, "Please help me, please help me while I sleep; please help me; please help me." You woke up the next day and it feels like, "I don't know; I just feel weird, or like a truck

---

*See Chapter 11 in this book.

Notes:

_____

_____

_____

ran over me. And somehow, after that meditation something just went away." Twenty years worth of something went away that you never even thought you could get through. You would have had to go through so many calamities in your life to wake you up. You would have gone through lifetimes worth of stuff that you would have had you take birth many lifetimes to get through – to wake you up over and over again, to get through it. That is why you have to pull on Gourasana and the special assistance: "Please, I don't know how I am going to get this wall down."

You are going to be in there in meditation sometimes trying to do it by yourself, and then you are going to re-member: "Oh, yeah, Gourasana, help me." You forgot to call on Him. You think you are in there doing it alone until you remember, "Oh, I have Gourasana." And you remember Him, although He is helping you anyway. He hears your prayer, even if you are calling on Him or not. He hears you and He is helping you. But once you connect again to Him and start pulling with Him, then the work goes really fast, and then you are right on the other side.

So the main point I want to give you is that when the illusion starts coming, don't run away from it. Don't wait to deal with it and procrastinate. Just say, "Okay, here it comes," and get your meditation gear ready. Finish up what you are doing and get ready, because you know you

Notes:

are going to be meditating. You might have to go to work or do this or that, but the other hours during the day you are going to be meditating until the wall moves.

Do not just meditate a little bit, but go after the walls now; you want to move them because you want your clarity and your connection back at the soonest possible moment. You don't want this thing lingering on.

The Importance of Meditation

Spoken on August 13, 2007

There are so many different components of spiritual transformation that need to be spoken about to those desiring ultimate union with God. There is one basic spiritual practice that everyone is trying to avoid or trying to get away with doing the minimal amount. And that is meditation. *You must meditate.*

A meditation that I am introducing is called *Cry, Heal, Pray.* In this meditation, you cry and pray and open up all of the parts inside of you that are stuck, and that are dark. You open up all the parts that are ego. You feel the sorrow, places where you are lost, areas of hate and blame and anger. There are so many things inside of you that need to be purged out of you, and these are a few examples. In this meditation, you go very deep within in a prayerful state, actually releasing those things as you are going deeper and deeper. You do not get stuck wallowing in these things, but you release them. This is a big part of the spiritual work.

Notes:

Then there is the ego and the breakdown of the ego and the meditation work that has to be done for breaking down the ego. You will spend hours on the floor looking at your ego. You have to have the awareness to see the ego and begin to break down the ego structure. (You will also go to workshops and seminars over years, breaking down the ego until you're willing to give up your ego entirely.) Eventually the true part of you comes through you fully; you just don't want that ego anymore, and you let it go. It is as simple as that with the ego. You see it and you are so sincere; you want the Lord so badly that you want to let go of your ego more than you want to hang on. And until that day comes, you suffer. Your ego can't get anywhere on this path but trapped. This transformation is a process of seeing the ego and understanding it so you can let go of it. It is a process of getting through the ego. And that takes a lot of meditation.

Then there is the meditation of longing to be with the Lord. In this meditation, your heart is opening up and being completely joined with the heart of God. You are feeling the Lord so much that your heart is just bursting in feeling the Lord. Then you are opening up to the Lord and to the Heavenly Host where you are filled with the holy energy of the Lord. You have many meditations like that, and when you do that, that energy of the Lord comes in to you and just wipes away the illusion in big chunks. It is very

Notes:
_____

_____

_____

powerful meditation when that energy can enter you and fill you with the presence of the Lord and, at the same time, destroy the illusion. That is very special help from God, and that does a lot of the work of destroying illusion when you can let that happen. It opens up all of your chakras at the same time.

You have to work hard in meditation. You need to have three powerful days of meditation each week. That is why it is set up to have weekly meditations at the meditation centers. The best thing is to have two 3-hour meditations a week and one longer, 12-hour meditation every week; I call these long meditation days "Go Deeper Days." These Go Deeper Days are when the Host can get in and work with everyone. This weekly meditation schedule is the ideal program for someone who wants to come Home.

You can't wait for a spiritual leader to guide a meditation in order to have a meditation. Meditation can happen in your bedroom, and in your house, together with the people you live with. Meditation at night for one hour is a very good thing. You have to be so connected to God every single second of every single day so you are just moving, moving, moving, moving, moving, moving, moving. You are moving through illusion, moving through darkness, getting a greater connection to God, every day, every day, every day. Every day you are moving more, moving more, moving more.

Notes:

_____

_____

_____

Make meditation a part of your daily life in addition to going to work, sharing the love with other people, doing your service for God, and making money for God. And all the while, you are going out and finding people that you can talk to about everything that you are finding with God, everything that is available to those who want God and transformation. You see, you give your whole life to God. *And for those who want to break the cycle of birth and death, you will not make it if you do not meditate in the way that I am describing: constantly begging, screaming, crying, going deep to find Him.* There will be time for work, for service, for funding the Mission, for talking with people about the path and what is being offered. It will be one whole life of ecstasy in God. And you will be breaking free, and you will know it because you will be moving spiritually like crazy.

Meditate, meditate, meditate. Go deeper. Go to the programs that are accurate for you, because that is where you get your really fast movement. *And don't ever forget that I said "meditate."* Your biggest tool is meditation. The greatest assistance that this earth has is the Heavenly Host, so when you meditate at night, you can sit there and pray to the Host to please, please help you. Pray for the Host to please, please help you to go fast and deeper, please break up your illusions and your ego; and then lie there and let the Host in. Go deep so that the energy of the Host can get in.

Notes:
_____

_____

_____

Just do that meditation for an hour each night where you are going deep and where the Host is just entering your body, where you can feel the Lord in your heart and you shed a tear.

Meditate!

Meditation of David

Spoken on June 28, 2007

I want to name this meditation the "David Meditation*." It is a simple meditation of the entry of Gourasana's energy. It is actually equally as important as the Modern-Day Meditation – the "Meditation for This Age."

When you get to a certain point in your spiritual transformation, you will tap into this meditation. You will have to do it every day at a certain point in your transformation as you mature spiritually. You will have to do it when it is a very heavy time spiritually; you feel a type of heaviness when Gourasana is filling you with the energy of the Lord.

In this meditation you are just lying on the floor, and you are just praying:

"Father, Father, Father, take me. Take me.
I want to come Home. I just want to come Home.
Please help me to give up my control.
Please help me to give up my ego.
Please help me to give up everything,

---

* Kalindi is naming this meditation in honor of David Swanson, the man who gave his life for Gourasana to come to this world. For more information, see *Definition of Names and Terms* in the back of the book.

Notes:
_____

_____

_____

75

because I only want to be with You. Please, Father,
help me. Please help me. Please help me. Please, please.
I beg of You to please help me to rid myself of all
of the things that separate me from You."

And while you are crying and praying this prayer,
the transformational energy from Gourasana will start to
enter you. As you are praying, the energy will be coming
into your body and moving through your body at a rapid
kind of rate, so you are vibrating very fast. And as you are
opening and crying in meditation, that energy can move
through your body and break up illusions. It can just break
them up, and they will just disappear. That energy will eventually be able to move through your entire body, and there
will be no blocks, all the chakras will be open, and all the
illusions will be gone.

People need to get started right away in doing this
meditation when they come to the Mission or the seminars
that we sponsor. This is very important for everyone to tap
into, even if they have no desire to go Home. Because if
people will open up enough so the Lord can move through
their bodies and bring them love and start to clear out
illusions, how wonderful it would be! How wonderful that
would be if people could learn what His energy feels like,
right from the start of their path.

Notes:
_____

_____

_____

People doing this transformational work need to open up like this once a week from the time they first start doing this work. It needs to be a weekly practice, because allowing the energy of the Lord to fill you is going to be the fastest way to have movement.

It is very, very important that you release your free will and your control and pray for help and mercy when you do this meditation. As you open more, then His energy can get in more and more and more.

In transformation, you will be going through periods of doing this deep meditation a lot. You will be in deep transformation, and Gourasana's energy will be coming in and in and in to you as you are crying and moving within that meditation. Sometimes it may happen for five days straight, morning and night. At those times, you will have the feeling that you can't wait until you get to meditation, because the energy is happening right now. Like at four o'clock in the morning, He could be waking you up to meditate. Surrender to doing those meditations, because He is taking you and moving you with the transformational energy going through you. He is killing off the illusion.

Start to meditate like this, and start to let Him come into you. Trust the movement in your body; trust when your legs start to feel like they are going to start to shake. Trust what your legs want to do and let them go. If you want to

Notes:
_____

_____

_____

pray to Gourasana, let Him in and pray, "Please, Gourasana, help me. Help me. Please take my free will; please take my control. I give it to You."

There is something that can happen when you stop your meditation and get up to go function in your life. Say you have meditated for two hours – that is a lot of light to take in – and then when you stand up and start functioning in your life, the light shines on the area where you stopped. It just keeps shining until it hits on any kind of shadow or darkness, and it shines on that darkness. Then you will get agitated. You might not know what it is even shining on; it is just some kind of block, and you become agitated. That is okay. You can just know that you are moving through something, but you will be able to function and you will be able to be nice to people.

But as soon as you can, get into a room where you can meditate and move through your feelings. It is just movement. You don't have to worry about identifying what it is along the way. You never even have to know what it is. You can just meditate and move through it. You can scream and meditate and move through whatever feelings or blocks are there. You can take that kind of path – that you never have to know what it is that you are moving through. You can just be a meditator and scream all the way through it very deeply and come out on the other side. And then a

Notes:

little while goes by, and then again you have to meditate and scream and move through it with the Lord's energy.

Meditating like this is an intense path, but I would be glad to teach anyone who would like to know that path. Don't be worried when you get into these situations where all of a sudden you are agitated or irritated. Just try to calm down. It will pass. The energy won't hurt you. It's benevolent. It just shakes in your body, and maybe you get a headache or stomachache*. Maybe your spine hurts a little, or you need to stretch, but you don't have to be afraid of the energy. Just invite it in and ask it to come in fast.

His energy, His transformational energy and special assistance are here to move us out of this illusion. You may not know what that special assistance is yet, but move forward and catch His energy as soon as you can.

I love you.

---

* Of course, if you have physical or medical symptoms, please see the appropriate medical professionals and do not assume that the energy is causing the symptoms.

Notes:

_____

_____

Call on the Name Gourasana

Spoken on March 20, 2007

Once you can find the presence of the Lord, that undeniable presence of the Lord, then through meditation you can keep going toward that presence more and more and more.

While you are feeling the presence of the Lord and going toward it more, that feeling of the presence itself is actually what is helping you to be able to keep going more and more into the presence of the Lord.

You have to cross through so many obstacles in your transformation, but first you go within into meditation *with* the Lord. You battle those obstacles with the presence of the Lord, with the focus on the Lord.

Meditate from a place of surrender, not resistance. Some of you may have to resist a little and that is okay, but the way to go into meditation is to go within *with* the presence of the Lord.

Once you have found the presence of the Lord, once you feel that presence, once you know that presence, then

Notes:

you know where you are going, because you are just going to let that feeling of presence come into you more and more. This will bring more and more of the love of God into you, for yourself and for everyone you meet. You will have more real true love of God. It is all hinged on going to the presence of the Lord. Go there. When you start meditation, focus and go there.

When you become calm, focus and go to the presence of the Lord; become calm and still in it.

When you become calm and still with the presence of the Lord, then so much information and understanding will be easily attainable and available to you.

Everyone has their connection with God. You can each feel your connection to a certain degree.

This path is meant to take you to a place where you are in complete love and ecstasy of being with the Lord.

So this is the focus – finding the presence of the Lord. It is all about you going into the presence more and more and more and finding your way to Him.

How do you do it? The answer is your path. That is your meditation. That is between you and God. Go within; go for the presence of the Lord. First thing is your desire. Second thing is prayer. Then never give up. Go very deep. Go very deep to the source of where the presence of the love is flowing from. Find it.

Notes:

_____

_____

For those of you that have the trust and faith, you can call on the name *Gourasana*. Calling on that name will hasten your journey. The presence of the Lord can be found faster and deeper when you call the name *Gourasana*. It will call the presence of the Lord to you as you go within.

When you think about finding the presence of the Lord more and more and more, then there is no room for all the issues and wallowing, because what do issues have to do with anything anyway? Issues all have to be given up, like a hot potato. You want the presence of the Lord, and the blocks that you are going to go through that are blocking you from that presence are bigger blocks than issues. Those blocks move with the presence of the Lord. Gourasana is specifically here to help you move through those blocks when it gets unbearable and you think you cannot do it. When you cannot go on, please call on His name over and over. Just call upon His name with your desire, and that block will move. You call on that name and that block will move, and you will move into more of the presence of the Lord.

Gourasana is an Incarnation of God. And He brings a special help. And one type of help is Himself. He is right there battling the fight with you to help you return fully to the presence of the Lord. When you think you just can't make it one more second, call upon His name. When you are trying to go so deep and you need help from the Lord –

Notes:

of course you can call on the Lord in any way that you want – but there is also Gourasana right with you, right now, with His special energy. He wants nothing else than for you to have the presence of the Lord and be in the love and ecstasy of that presence. He has come to help you.

If you want His special assistance that He is ushering in, then calling Gourasana's name is a good way to go. It's not necessary to call on His name; I say that because there are newcomers. If you don't have a connection with Him, or if you don't really call from your heart, or if you just start saying the name without the deepest heartfelt feeling, then it's useless just to say His name. People should not just call the name from some surface place. It is a deep thing to call upon His name. I don't want this to be a Mission that is running around calling on Gourasana, if it's not truly felt deeply within. But now I am releasing the name, "Gourasana." He is here to help you fight the illusions that you have to fight. He is here to help you to find and have a deeper and deeper and deeper connection with God.

The Core* transformed for many years, and David Swanson went through his transformation for many years, before he trusted to call upon the name Gourasana. But in the end of his transformation, one of the last steps he

---

* The Core is the group of seven people who founded this Mission with Gourasana. David Swanson is the man who gave his life so that Lord Gourasana could manifest in this world.

Notes:

needed to take in his transformation was to call on the name *Gourasana*. And that is when everything happened for him and the Mission started. The power poured in. When David called on the name *Gourasana*, he was so determined. He had complete trust and faith. At a certain point, calling on the name *Gourasana* was a very specific thing that David and the Core had to do. It took us three or four years to do it, but when we did, everything moved massively.

I am giving you the name *Gourasana* to call on now. In times when you need Gourasana, He is right there with you. Just as God is right there with you, Gourasana is right there. When you feel one, you will also feel the other. When you feel Gourasana, you will feel the presence of the Lord; and when you feel the Lord, you will feel the presence of Gourasana. A special thing that an Incarnation does is to bring that presence of the Lord to the world. It is so that you can feel more God and have more of God.

Good luck and never give up!

Notes:

Going Into Meditation with Gourasana

By Savanna Cassidy

September 6, 2007

Kalindi: *I've always said that through the endeavor and transformation of the first 100 people that came to Miracle of Love, the path would be easier for those who would come after them. This is a talk and teaching from a disciple in that group who has been on the "freer and freer" path. I'm very proud of her and of all of my first disciples. She has figured out in words what goes on when you do the meditation work on the floor with Gourasana, with the Host assisting you – what actually happens. This is just the beginning of so many teachers and so many masters speaking the truth and teachings from their own realized state.*

Savanna: Once you have chosen to surrender to Gourasana and you have trust and faith in Him, this is really important to know and remember: When you go into meditations in which you are doing deep work to let go and completely sever places where you are bound and attached, you have to

Notes:

85

go into your meditation *with Gourasana.* You have to bring Gourasana into your meditation. That is what He is here for. That is what His transformational energy and His special assistance are here for.

When you are doing this type of meditation – the deep work of letting go to sever your attachments – at times you are going to be hitting up against something that, no matter how hard you try or what you do, you somehow can't quite fully get to the bottom of it and know that it is gone. In this type of meditation, two things have to be happening simultaneously. The first thing is that you have to be a hundred percent willing to give it up. You have to be a hundred percent willing to face what you have to face, feel what you have to feel, be completely honest, have no denial, have no repression. You have to find that place of a hundred percent "yes." And it only takes a split second for that hundred percent "yes" to happen. There is just a feeling that happens where you just know "Okay, this is it, I'm going for it. And I'm going to just go through this meditation and I'm going to just give it up, one thing after the next. Here, take this, take this, take this." You will know very consciously that there is not one part of you that is holding on. Then as you are meditating, you can start just letting it go. As it comes up in your meditation, you go through what you have to go through. You feel what you have to feel.

Notes:
_____

_____

_____

And then you come to a point where you know, "Okay, good, now it's gone," So one thing that has to happen is your one hundred percent "yes."

Then the second thing that has to happen is that you need to let Gourasana in, one hundred percent. You have to know that you have complete trust and faith in Him and that you invite Him in, in your meditation. You let Him in to do His part. You will go through whatever He takes you through. And you are just constantly praying for "More, more, more. Take me. Take me." And you just let Him take you – within.

Those two things have to come together simultaneously. And when that happens, then you're on your way. You are doing your work and you are letting go. Where you get tripped up in meditation is that you are either not a hundred percent willing to let go of what you are holding on to, or you are not letting Him in one hundred percent.

You could be letting Gourasana completely in, completely taken by His energy. You need to know that He is within working with you, and you are surrendered to that. But there's a part of you that won't completely give up what you are holding on to. So you have to find that hundred percent "yes." Then the other side, where you get tripped up is you are actually completely a hundred percent "yes," and you're wanting to let go fully and you're wanting to feel everything and you're wanting to walk away, but you're

Notes:

_____

_____

not letting Gourasana in all the way. You're trying to do it on your own. You don't have enough trust and faith in God. And you're not letting Him in all the way, so He can do His work.

You have to find these two things, and then everything can happen for you in meditation in a split second. You do not even have to struggle. You just have to give Him permission, and you have to give yourself permission. And then it's all about your trust and faith, knowing that it is completely possible. Then you just go with Him.

In coming to a one-hundred-percent willingness, there is an absolute knowing that comes in a split second, just a "yes." Otherwise, when you're in meditation and you're praying and you're praying, and you are letting Gourasana completely in and know that He's taking you over, and you trust His energy, but instead you have this feeling, it's a struggle: "Why won't it go away? Why won't it go away? I'm asking, please take it, please take it," there is one part of you that won't give it up. And you can't really understand why it's not going away no matter how hard you try.

On your side of the work, you just need to be honest about everything and find this complete hundred percent letting go. You must have your hundred percent "Yes; take it, take it, take me through everything that I have to feel." You are just going, going, going and you are just giving, giving,

Notes:

giving and you are just letting go. At the same time, Gourasana is a hundred percent doing His part because you've invited Him in. You are not in your mind. You have completely let Him take you, and His transformational energy and special assistance are working in you. As you let go to that, the two of those together will completely help you, and you come to the place where you are letting go. You are not just having a breakthrough, but you are actually severing attachments. You are letting go at a very deep level so you are no longer bound by these things that you were bound by.

Have a very conscious meditation. While you are in your meditation and you are completely letting Gourasana take you, you don't get lost in the energy; you are not tripping out in the energy, but you know that you are completely in it. You have opened up your body, you are letting Him in, and you are just moving with His energy. You are also giving a hundred percent. Then your mind can be very conscious.

In a way, you are letting go to His energy and you are not tripping out in it, but you have let go of your mind control and are using your mind now in a very conscious way. You are paying attention to what it is that you are working on. You are right there talking to Gourasana. You are telling Him what it is. You are letting go of what you need to let go of. There may be words like, "Here, please take this illusion." And, "Oh my God, I can't believe I have

Notes:

_____

_____

to feel that, but okay, here I go." And you just keep facing it and feeling it. You are letting go rapid speed, one thing after the next. You face it, you feel it, you let go. It is your conscious giving, your conscious awareness of what's going on. It's your conscious knowing of "I've got to go a little bit further; there's something else," or "Please, Gourasana, show me where else there is to go." You are making sure that you have covered the whole area that you need to cover. Then He just gets in there with His transformational energy and His special assistance and it's just sever, sever, sever, letting go, letting go, letting go.

It is a totally conscious meditation. That is why you are going to know that you have actually gotten through something. And you know that you have let go. You have seen it for what it is, you faced the feelings around it, and you know that you've let go. You are going to feel it in your body. You will just feel different. It is not like a breakthrough, where you just have this breakthrough and you get real high. It's deeper than a breakthrough. It's a very deep subtle feeling that carries a lot of light.

This is the way that you need to meditate when you know you have to get free from the things that have you bound. You need to have your hundred percent desire to let go, and you need to have a hundred percent trust and faith and surrender to let Gourasana do His part.

Notes:
_____

_____

_____

Remember This

Spoken on February 3, 2008

This talk deserves to be called *"Remember This,"* because you are going to forget it. You are going to forget it so many times, especially the very first time that you experience a day when, all of a sudden, you do not feel so good in your consciousness and in your mind, and of course, your body follows suit. The biggest thing will be the agitation in your mind followed by the absence of the light. You will not know what is going on. It starts to get dark within. You cannot feel God; it gets darker and darker within, and it goes on day after day, week after week. It gets worse and worse until there is nothing but darkness followed by no hope whatsoever. You do not tell anybody about it, because you do not know what is happening. You have been completely covered over by the darkness.

As you get closer and closer to God, this is going to happen, and it happens because there is so much light. The light shines so intensely on the darkness, and the closer you get to God, the more you start to go back Home through the separation – that original separation from when you first left the true realm. There is a space of complete darkness be-

Notes:

tween you and God that happens from the original fall when you first separated from God. You have to go back through that darkness into the arms of God, all the way Home.

As you are doing that part of your transformation of going through the original separation from God, you are going to go through a period of so much darkness. But every time you go through that darkness and you win each battle with the darkness and you come out into the light, there is more glory of God and more shining bright light. You will feel an inner light; it is not an actual light shining, but you will feel an inner light inside you. There is so much consciousness, awareness, and even ecstasy when this happens. You come to a point where there is no darkness going on within you, and you feel so free. (It feels like this every time you get through a big battle with darkness within.) Then there will be a period of time before you go through another battle like that again. Every time you go through it and come out the other side, there will be more God, more light, and more love.

I am telling you, *"Remember This,"* because when the darkness comes, you are going to forget this will happen and what to do. The biggest thing you are going to forget is to get to your meditation spot and meditate as soon as you can. It is going to be the last thing you want to do, but it is the thing that you need to do because you need to push back the illusion. You need to go through the dark tunnel.

Notes:

_____

_____

_____

You have to just push away the dirt and keep going, because somehow you know that on the other side of that dirt, the Lord is waiting and has come to take you Home. You have to scream and you have to cry and you have to call on the name of the Lord and just go through the darkness. You have to remember that.

Please remember this. You are going to hit into a place that is so bad and so separate, and this is because you are going back through the darkness into the Lord. He is waiting there with His hands out to take you Home. When you hit these dark places, you need to do your meditation and call on the Lord! Just put on the Gourasana talk where He says to pray out loud*, because you are going feel some very dark things deep within. Remember that these things are not you. They are just feelings.

You are going to feel some pretty horrible things within that you cannot avoid, so you can always scream. If you want to get mad at God when you are in this place, go ahead. Do whatever you have to do in that meditation. Do it and move through it. Now *Remember This:* When this happens, when that feeling of separation or darkness or feeling bad comes, get on the meditation floor as soon as possible and go through it. *You must meditate. You must.* If you do not meditate, there is no possibility for success.

---

* See Chapter 11 in this book.

Notes:

_____

_____

_____

GIVE UP YOUR ISSUES

*The Only
Solution
to the Problem
Is to
Go Deeper.*

GOURASANA

Drop Issues Like a Hot Potato

Spoken on February 18, 2008

Gourasana gave us a very simple path to follow, and it is how I guided The Lady and the whole Core* since the beginning of Miracle of Love. That is the path Home.

Since then, people have taken so much time to dig to the bottom of all their stuff within. The problem is, they just do not want to let go. The only problem is hanging on. And the only solution to any problem that one may find on their path – the only solution to anything – is to go deeper.

People on the path have to stop insisting on reconciling the material and squeezing it into the spiritual. Gourasana said that process of trying to reconcile material issues will go on forever. The only solution to any problem that one may find on their path is to go deeper. Because once you go deeper, you will find the Lord. It may take a couple of hours of meditating and crying and perhaps even screaming, or even just calming for hours, until you find Him. But once you find Him, He is the one that is going to guide your way.

---

* The Core is the group of seven people who founded this Mission with Gourasana and Kalindi.

Notes:

_____

_____

_____

He is going to tell you what to do and what you need to work on.

The deeper you get and the closer to Him that you get, the more you are going to be able to hear Him say, "Come this way. Do this." And if you don't do what He says, He is going to stop talking to you until you do what He says to do. But, if you meditate with the desire to find Him, there will be no lack of understanding what He wants you to do. "Lord, please, where are You? I need to talk to You, I need Your help, please." The solution to all the problems is to meditate deeper and deeper and deeper and find that connection to Him. And of course, at some point, you will have that connection, and you will know where to go to find Him and how to stay with Him.

That is the spiritual work: to find Him and then stay with Him. And do whatever you can to stay with Him. Don't let the three most obvious signs of the illusion get you: don't let negative thinking, judgments, or discouragement get you.

You are going to go through many hard times on your path. If you stop engaging with the smaller issues like I am telling you, then the bigger obstacles are going to be there. For example, all of a sudden you find that you are really angry. You are really angry because you are facing something inside of you that is causing you to have great anger, but you don't even know what it is. That is not an issue. It is deep-

Notes:

rooted and bigger than a small issue of being angry about a surface thing. You might even go for three weeks just angry, but you don't dare put it out on anybody else. Just deal with it in meditation. Or just sit in your room and just be angry.

The only solution to your problem is to go deeper. When you do this, you are not going to be able to sit there in your mind and think about your issues; as soon as you go deeper, your issues are going to disappear, because your issues are on the surface. And your issues are all of the illusion. If you're going to play around with your issues, no matter what they are, then you are playing in the illusion. *Go deeper.* And if you have an issue that is so difficult and just driving you crazy, then you can go to a spiritual leader, or you can get help in some way.

If you are going to work on issues, then it is going to be one issue after the other after the other, because the illusion knows that is how it can get you: "Let's bring up more – here more – here more - here more, more, more, more, more." Drop those issues! No issues! That is the path that The Lady walked and the Core walked. Gourasana was sitting there seeing to it that we did it that way. He didn't care about those issues. He is here to take you Home, and "You better come fast, faster than the illusion can get you." You need to go to God faster then the illusion can get you.

Notes:
_____

_____

_____

98

"Faster than the illusion can get you" means *you drop the issue like a hot potato.* It doesn't matter what the issue is! You can work on the bigger things. For example, if you are going through a divorce, that is an issue that is going to take you a while to heal. But if somebody bothers you every time you see her because you don't like the way she smiles and she has this edge about her and you think she doesn't like you and it bothers you every day when you go to work – well, that's just too bad. That's just too bad! Get over it. Change your job. But do something about it right now, because it's stopping you from going to God. It's stopping you from going to God. *It's stopping you from going to God.* Get rid of it.

Don't hold on. Read the Saint Francis prayer and also the "Fruits of the Holy Spirit,"*and start to live by those things.

Again, Gourasana said the process of issues will go on forever. There are endless issues because there are endless lifetimes. And once you have completely finished working on the issues of this lifetime, then you are going to start to feel other things. And those things will be coming into you from previous lifetimes, and you will start working on something that you don't even know what it is, but you will start working on it and you will come up with something that warrants going to a Seminar and going through, "What is this thing?" No!

---

* These quotations are included in Chapter 19, "*Cry for God, Not Your Issues.*"

Notes:

_____

_____

_____

You have to have desire for God that is greater than your issues that are driving you crazy. And when you go to the foot of your bed every night, throw your issues in your garbage bag: Imagine having a trash bag there, and throw all your issues into that bag before you go to sleep. Every single thing that has been bothering you all day long, throw it in the bag.

You have to know how to go deeper and deeper within. When it is like a black tunnel within, in meditation you have to just claw your way through whatever is in the way until you can see the light again. You just have to keep going. Sometimes it is very dark, but you have to keep going and going and going, and the light will be there. You cannot stop until that light is there and the illusion is at bay.

One disciple hit the tunnel of darkness and forgot that I said to go *through* that tunnel. In meditation, you have to get on your hands and knees and go through that tunnel screaming for Gourasana, begging for Gourasana out loud, "Lord, please help me." She forgot this, and she felt like she couldn't move out of her chair for three weeks. She said it felt like there was no light. There was no God. There was nothing. She sat there for three weeks, and she did not get on the floor and do that meditation screaming for Gourasana. She just thought everything was lost; she thought it was just all gone. She forgot everything and she

Notes:

didn't remember that I said, "Use the *How to Pray** talk from Gourasana and get down there on the floor, meditate, and dig your way through that tunnel within. Because now you're going to face the separation from God." It feels like you are crossing back through the separation from God, and it is dark. It feels like you are crossing through the original separation, the fall from God, and it is nothing but dark.

The Lady just knew, "I have to let go," and she knew there was no way she was going to try to hang on to an issue. She just heard Gourasana's words, "You must let go. And you must meditate. And you have to go deeper. And now you have to go deeper." And the path that The Lady walked, worked.

Everyone has a lot to get through, so now get through it on the floor. Get through it on the floor. Meditate, meditate, meditate, meditate!

---

* See Chapter 11 in this book.

Notes:

_____

_____

_____

Cry for God, Not Your Issues

The Lady Speaking on April 14, 2008
at The Intensive

In the beginning of our life in the Core with Gourasana in 1987, He told us He wanted to meditate with people who were going to let go and go within to the presence of the Lord. He didn't tell us *how* to do that; He just said that we were going to meditate and go within to the presence of the Lord. Then He began leading meditations and guiding us within to the presence of the Lord.

During that period, there were times when Gourasana would ask people to meditate in a different room, because they were having a hard time, and there were things they needed to address that were obstacles in the way of going within to the presence of the Lord. Then it happened to me. I was also asked to meditate elsewhere because I was internally upset, shut down, resistant, angry, and stuck in my issues. So when time came for meditation, Gourasana asked me to leave the room where He was and go meditate in another room. (I call that other room "the issue box" room.)

Notes:

I was mortified, embarrassed, and felt humiliated – which made me even more shut down, stuck, upset, resistant, and angry. I was in a very shabby state of consciousness and clearly stuck in the habit of dealing with issues.

I remember sitting on the floor with my legs out in front of me and my arms closed over my chest, stuck and perplexed, wondering, "What do I do? How do I do it?" I definitely did not like being in the issue box room. I was thrown within to face myself: What do I want? Is what I am doing bringing me closer to God or not? I knew I wanted to be with Him, and *that* wanting, that desire to be with Him is what finally made me start to crack, crumble, and bleed for Him. Then my heart finally broke open, and I was moving through the anger, resistance, and rigid habits, all out of desire for Him. My strong desire was able to crack through that shabby state of consciousness I began with and get me moving beyond and deeper than the issues. Desire for Him moved me to Him. It then took several hours of meditating with serious longing, fervent prayers to get free, and letting go before I was open and deep enough to again be with Gourasana.

Several hours later I sat with Gourasana, and He asked, "Well Lady, did you let go?"

"Yes Gourasana, I did."

Through this experience, I learned two things about meditation that were critical for me. The first is that no

Notes:
_____

_____

_____

matter what terrible state I was in at the beginning of meditation, if I wanted to be in God's room, I could change that illusory energy with decision, desire, longing, prayer, and letting go.

Secondly, I learned that if I remained in the issues of the mind and stayed resistant, angry, stuck, embarrassed, and mortified, I could not move toward God. And I was wasting precious, valuable time by spinning in the hamster wheel of illusions and issues.

I felt humbled by this experience, and that was a good thing, because it reminded me to keep my head at the feet of the Lord.

Very simply, if you want union with God, then you need to go within, release emotions, let go, and pray sincerely for the Lord. That's all that I did.

Most people don't yet understand how to meditate properly and how to let go of issues. They must understand that crying in the issues is very distinct from crying for the Lord. People mistakenly believe that crying in the issues will somehow get them closer to God. It will not, because crying in the issues is crying in the illusion's room. But if you are crying unconditionally from your soul for God, you are not in the illusion's room, and that is the cry that God can hear.

So if you want God, meditate for God. If you keep meditating on the issues of what goes on in this plane of

Notes:

illusion, you will become lost in that process for a very long time, because there are endless issues, just as there are endless lifetimes to keep focusing on these endless issues. Examples of issues are agitation, overwhelm, unworthiness, negative thoughts, judgments, jealousy, envy, blaming others, arrogance, laziness, fear, neediness, self-absorption, resentment, anger – the issues are endless.

Kalindi tells us that once you have completely finished working on the issues of this lifetime, then you are going to start to feel and work on issues from previous lifetimes. Now, what about *that* trick of the illusion! – getting you to work on issues from previous lifetimes when the past does not really even exist. The past and the future are also illusions, and to use precious time to resolve or heal the issues of past or future is an example of the insidious traps that keep you bound to this plane of illusion.

When taking issues into meditation as a focus, you are definitely not in the present, striving for God; you are in your being of illusion, with its endless worries, concerns, and issues. So does it really matter what your parents did to you when you were a child? You are no longer a child! You are an adult and your reality is not that of a child any longer. Stop working on issues of the past! If you stay trapped in healing or resolving all the traumatic and disturbing issues of the past, you are bound to the illusion of the past.

Notes:

Rather, take the approach, "The only solution to the problem is to go deeper." What does this essential principle of transformation tell you? It means that problems and issues come from the illusory false self, which is on the surface of your being. Your soul is deeper; your soul encompasses the true part of you that is longing, crying, and begging to God to be free. The true part of you is humility, is prayer, and is the desire to return Home.

So when you go deeper, it means you are not going to be able to be stuck in the mind and think about your issues; as soon as you go deeper, the issues are going to disappear. The issues are from the being of illusion – the false personality and the ego – and the issues are *all* of the illusion. If you are going to insist on working through issues – no matter what they are – then you are trapped and bound in the material world of illusion, and there you will continue to stay working on issue after issue, lifetime after lifetime … until you finally let go, give up, and surrender to God.

Gourasana didn't care about my issues or my angry feelings because they were of the illusion. He held a higher purpose for me. He was here to take me Home, and I had better let go fast, or I would take another birth. That is what I was presented with – very simple. The same choice is before you now.

As far as I'm concerned, this entire world and what is going on here is one gigantic "issue box," and basically everyone is trapped in its horror show. Everyone. My son used to come to my house after work, and he would have to spend an hour or more talking to me about the issues and insanity of the work place – "This person did this and that person did that, and that and that" – just to get stable again; just to be sane again. You turn on TV and watch CNN and it's one dark dramatic issue box. You are viewing one tragic issue after another, after another, after another, after another, after another, with no resolution and no hope.

I gave you a sign that said: "It Is God That Is Happening." Once I started transformation, I knew it was God that was happening, and to put it another way, I knew Gourasana was an Incarnation of God. I held on to that fact throughout the darkest times. I also knew Kalindi was not only speaking the truth, but she was guiding me to find the truth within. In fact, Kalindi was speaking the truth *constantly* and guiding us to the next step to get disentangled from the illusion. I knew Gourasana and Kalindi wanted to help as many people as possible graduate from this plane of illusion. I knew that somehow or other my destiny was to stand strong with Kalindi and Gourasana, which meant I had to let go and go fast – faster than the illusion could get me. If you're not moving fast, you are in the illusion. So I had to let go, go deeper, go faster, and go to Him over and over – and that was my path.

Notes:

So it's time for you to let go, to go deeper, to go faster than the illusion can get you, and it's time for you to find Him – completely.

The issues are stopping you from getting God.
The issues are stopping you from going to God.
The issues are stopping you from having God.

Get rid of the issues. You drop the issues like a hot potato to go deeper. That's what it means when we say: *"The only solution to the problem is to go deeper."*

The Ten No's – And Other Tools to Keep You Out of Issues

The Ten No's are a list of illusions *not* to engage with so you can go deeper into God consciousness or awareness. They are:

1. No Assumption or Speculation
2. No Hearsay
3. No Rumor
4. No Gossip
5. No Discouragement
6. No Judgments
7. No Negative Thinking
8. No Wallowing
9. No Complaining
10. No Issues

Notes:

Can you just imagine what the world would be like without the Ten No's running rampant? And can you imagine how much more genuine love, care, and respect could be present amongst people without the Ten No's?

No assumption or speculation. You really have to start practicing Gourasana's teaching: "Think before you speak." Pray before you speak. Meditate before you speak.

No hearsay. No gossip. No rumor. Kalindi has said to me, "Lady, I want gossip to stop. There are people in the Mission who are still gossiping." So I ask you how are you going to stop gossip? Stop now – is how you do it! And a motivating factor is to realize the damage and hurt people suffer as a result of gossip, including the damage to your own consciousness.

No discouragement. Discouragement is a closed-hearted, self-absorbed position of looking at the glass half empty – which shuts God out. Discouragement is the opposite of *Everything Is Possible with God*. *Everything Is Possible with God* is an openhearted, giving position that allows possibility and movement in the flow of God.

No judgments of others. Always imagine walking in another person's footsteps to see and feel what it's like for that person. Earnest spiritual seekers must attain this

Notes:

unique ability. Isn't that what Jesus meant when He guided us to "Love one another"? Jesus' guidance was universal. I don't think Jesus meant to love only your own family or country. Judgments are the illusion's poison, and judging others is not the path Jesus desired for people to follow. To understand this further, meditate on Gourasana's talk *"The Beautiful Gem."**

No negative thinking, no wallowing, no issues, no complaining. David Swanson** did not complain. From my perspective, how dare anyone complain about any of the hardships necessary in the transformation back Home to God! Drop these Ten No's like a hot potato. They are reason for rebirth, because they are from the illusion. Break the bad habit of being trapped in issues. Walk away from this world's issue box. When you think about it, when you really spend some time thinking about it, you will see how many atrocious problems and how much unnecessary suffering would be remedied if people would gain mastery over themselves in these areas. "There is nothing sweeter than control," said Gourasana. And for the people on this Path, mastery in this area is required for union with God. The issues are in the way of your loving relationship with God and with people.

---

*Gourasana's "The Beautiful Gem" talk is available at www.miracle.org.
** David Swanson is the man who gave his life so that Lord Gourasana could manifest in this world.

Notes:

Turning away from the illusions of the Ten No's causes you to turn toward God, to think about God more, and to love God more. In turn, your awareness is increasing because you are in action practicing the presence of God. You just have to do it. You just have to become aware and do it.

Think before you speak. Pray before you speak. Meditate before you speak. Listen carefully to yourself while you are speaking to people. Become aware of when you are speaking from judgment or negativity so you can stop it in the moment. When you stop it in the moment, there will be a positive shift in your consciousness, and you will not be contaminating others' minds and hearts with your judgments and negativity. This is how you care for people. Turn away from the illusions of this world, and never look back; catch yourself in the moment and just turn away. Become aware; become fully aware, then you will be able to listen and to hear His whispers in the sound of silence inside of you and to feel His care for people.

In addition to saying no to the Ten No's, Kalindi wants you to practice the guidance in "Why Were the Saints, Saints?" The guidance in this quote is one of the ways to start gaining some mastery over the illusion's world of the Ten No's by practicing the qualities of the saints.

Notes:
_____

_____

_____

Why Were the Saints, Saints?

Because they were cheerful
When it was difficult
To be cheerful,
Patient when it was difficult
To be patient,
And because they pushed on
When they wanted to stand still,
And kept silent
When they wanted to talk,
And they were agreeable
When they wanted to be disagreeable.
THAT WAS ALL!
It was quite simple and
Always will be.

MIRIAM C. HUNTER

Kalindi also wants you to practice the "St. Francis Prayer":

Saint Francis Prayer

Lord, make me an instrument of Thy peace;
where there is hatred, let me sow love;
where there is injury, pardon;
where there is doubt, faith;
where there is despair, hope;
where there is darkness, light;
and where there is sadness, joy.

O Divine Master,
grant that I may not so much seek to be consoled
as to console;
to be understood, as to understand;
to be loved, as to love;
for it is in giving that we receive,
it is in pardoning that we are pardoned,
and it is in dying that we are born to Eternal Life.

Amen

FRANCIS OF ASSISI,
13TH CENTURY

Kalindi wishes for you to embrace the "Fruits of the Holy Spirit":

Fruits of the Holy Spirit

Love

Joy

Peace

Patience

Kindness

Generosity

Faithfulness

Gentleness

Self-Control

GALATIANS 5: VERSE 22,
NEW TESTAMENT

And I would like you to let go to the "Serenity Prayer":

༐

The Serenity Prayer

God,
Grant me the serenity to accept things I cannot change,
Courage to change things I can, and
Wisdom to know the difference.

REINHOLD NIEBUHR

Kalindi said, "Whoever thought they could have union with God without all of these?"

Now you know what to let go of, and you know what will replace the bad habits of issues and illusion. When you follow the direction of these four pieces of inspiration, you will be practicing the presence of God.

David Swanson on Issues and the Illusion

How did David Swanson deal with issues and the illusion? Well, about worry, he simply said, "Don't worry."

About negative thoughts he said, "Think positively; know you can change."

About being tired he said, "You are tired because you are swimming against the current."

About gossip he said, "Never criticize anyone. Develop patience, tolerance, and have compassion."

About discouragement he said, "Gain a success attitude. Focus on what you want and go after it."

About judgments he said, "Acting poorly toward others is an offense toward God," and "Everyone is more important than you are."

In addition David said, "Make a list of the obstacles between you and success."

"Get in touch with the Lord and you will be given the power to succeed."

"Think and be specific."

"Remove negative thoughts."

"Never be timid."

"Come up with substitutes for bad habits."

"Don't let laziness affect your projects from being done well."

"A favor done poorly is almost an insult."

Notes:

My Points on Issues:

Number one: I had to see that when I allowed myself to be caught in the Ten No's, I was choosing to suffer by my attachment to being angry, resistant, and rigid rather than letting go. It took me a while to understand what Gourasana meant when he told me that I was attached to suffering.

Number two: I understood Gourasana when He said: "Everyone has the same problem and that is they are in illusion." I understood that we are all lost in a world where every person suffers and every person has issues that are tragic; and I understood that we are all trapped in a world that is alien to our true nature, because it is not our true Home. I understood that the biggest problem was my separation from God. Therefore my problems, illusions, issues, and wounds were basically no greater and no less than anyone else's. I understood that if I wanted to focus on healing the issues and wounds of my life I would miss out on God. I wanted God; I sought for God; I fought for God; and I found that it is only the love and truth of God that could heal my broken heart.

Number three: The majority of people's speaking is from the Ten No's. The Ten No's are not coming from awareness, or from a consciousness that truly loves and cares for others, loves and accepts oneself, and loves God.

Notes:

_____

_____

Number four: I realized that I am the one who is responsible for my own states of consciousness: not other people; not the condition of the world; not whether there is war or peace, death or life, strife or happiness; not the things I have or have not; not the past or the future. I alone am responsible for my own states of consciousness.

Number five: Gourasana said, "Practically speaking, there is nothing but garbage in your minds." Contemplating those words, I then thought, how could I take the garbage of my mind so seriously? The mind is part of the illusory self; the mind is filled with the garbage of illusion; so I could no longer be so seriously engaged with the noise of the mind. I had to go deeper to detach from the garbage and see it as false, as illusion. I had to go deeper to truly begin to listen to the sound and guidance of silence.

Number six: Be calm. I am constantly working toward becoming calmer, becoming detached, and becoming equipoised.

Number seven: Remember the bigger picture. One of my strengths is that I *do* always remember the bigger picture.

Remember the bigger picture and turn to Him.
Remember the bigger picture and let go with awareness.
Remember the bigger picture and turn away
from the ways of this world.

Notes:
_____

_____

_____

Number eight: Become determined to rapidly change and to let go. I have experienced the determination of Kalindi. I have never experienced anyone more determined than Kalindi. When Kalindi becomes aware of something that needs to be changed, she makes the change practically in the moment, and she does it with determination. Then Kalindi keeps up the momentum necessary for rapid change and letting go. Kalindi is awake. Kalindi is aware. And Kalindi is a vibrant living example of what it means to live in the present. It is stunning to be a witness to such rapid transformation. An example: Only one time in meditation did Kalindi cry in an issue. David heard Kalindi and told her something like "That is not the type of crying that will get you closer to God," and Kalindi stopped what she was doing in that meditation in the moment. God says "change" and Kalindi changes; God says, "let go" and Kalindi lets go. Everyone should strive to follow Kalindi's example: Become determined to change and let go in the moment.

Also, this quality of determination overcomes the negative thoughts and discouragement that have people stagnate and prevent them from letting go and changing rapidly.

Two Other Important Points
Using the Modern-Day Meditation. Please don't think I'm saying "Don't release the emotions." If you are caught in the emotions of an issue, you have to use the Modern-Day

Notes:

_____

_____

_____

Meditation. Use the Modern-Day Meditation and release the emotions. And everyone has the big obstacles that bring up deep feelings that must be released. My big obstacle was anger, which included other illusions that were attached to anger, such as self-absorption, repression, and unworthiness. Anger was the big obstacle that kept the separation from God in place. By addressing the big obstacles, you are simultaneously weakening other illusions, becoming freer from them. You do not have to individually work through each and every illusion. But if you want to get free, you have to go through the big illusions all the way – while letting them go. And you must release deep feelings in Part One of the Modern-Day Meditation. With practice, your ability to see the illusion and let go with awareness will increase.

Getting professional help. If you have traumatizing issues or addictions that are blocking your transformation, then you need to get professional medical or psychological help for the specific problem; we can't help you with that, because this work is spiritual. Set a time frame for completion.

Conclusion

About the Ten No's, remember this:

The real problem is that you are not letting go.

That is the only problem.

So be finished with the Ten No's

Notes:

Please –

Let this be the last time we talk about this!

Find your way!

    Become an example

       for others to find their way.

    Let us all allow the Presence of God

       by letting go, going deeper

         and actively practicing the Presence of God

          to be with God.

Notes:

Perception Is King

Jim St. James
Speaking on April 18, 2008
at The Intensive

I really am glad that The Lady declared, "No issues." And I have a story and a lesson today for you about that. The story is about myself. The lesson is what I learned, and it's for you. It has to do with issues and my path. It's been twenty years that I have been on my spiritual path. And the last time I talked to Kalindi, about two or three weeks ago, I had just gotten through a hard time, and I told her, "Yeah, I had a hard time and I did this and did that and got through it." And she said, "So that's how you do it?" I think it had always been a little bit of a mystery to her about how I get through a rough spot, because I would kind of disappear. Recently she said, "You should share this with the people, because there might be some people who are drawn to do it the same way you did it." So that is what I will do today.

So what would happen is I would get stuck. I would have an onset of emotions that would just come on. I would get triggered in some way, and probably ninety-nine out of a hundred times, it was from something Kalindi said or something I heard that she was planning to do, like a plan for the organization or something like that. When this onset of emotions would happen, I would be very surprised, because it was like night and day; I am fine one minute, and then either I'm reading a memo or hearing an update or something, and then the emotions come on. It was very annoying. It really felt like "This is the biggest trigger point possible." There are all other kinds of things that might come up that I'd get feelings about, but then that one trigger point where it really hits the core, let's say: that's what it felt like.

And what would happen is I would stop feeling my sense of normalcy, my sense of connection with God, the strength of my connection. I would be aware that my connection was there, but I wouldn't be feeling it, or I wouldn't be feeling it as strongly depending upon what the trigger was. I would get lost, and I could not find my way to let go of whatever was bothering me.

I would start to panic, not freak-out running-around panic, but my world would sort of start to crumble. It felt like all of a sudden my grip on reality was just knocked out from under me. This is kind of how it went my whole path. I progressed year after year into dealing with it a little better. And just in the last year, I feel like I have finally found out how to deal with it properly.

Notes:

I would lose my perspective. Nothing would make sense any more. When things make sense to me, my purpose is clear; my days have some meaning to them; I can have conversations freely; I can access laughter. You know, normal things like that. But when I was triggered, that would all go away, and it would get worse and worse and worse. And then some point early on in my transformation, I would start feeling like "I want to leave. I want to leave the Mission. I want to leave the Path." Just leave; leave the environment.

The way I thought about it, my perception of it, was that I have to leave the "sameness" of what we are doing. There was a feeling of, "We're doing the same thing. And I have to get away from it." I believed that it was the "sameness" that was causing my problem. This was the underlying premise that was going on in my mind.

But really what was happening was that each time I was thinking this, each time I was triggered, it was that my perspective was off. I would lose perspective. I would start to feel like I needed to be alone, because that was actually the only way I could feel safe. Safety was a thing for me. That was what my mind was saying, "I just don't feel safe." Not that I felt like anybody was going to attack me, but I think I didn't feel safe from within my own mind.

Notes:

_____

_____

It was like I didn't know my own sense of what is real and what is not. I think it was coming more from inside, and I would think, "I just have to go find some place and then I can feel safe. If I could just sit down and not have any people around me, have no input, no questions, no love, no care, no anything, then I can deal with that. I can take my next step. If I am unable to let go on the spot, then the next best thing is to remove myself, because I don't want my world to be this way any more."

It started off very awkwardly twenty years ago when I would do this. I'd lock myself in the room and not come out. And in the last year, I got to the point where I could say to my wife, "I'm going into my room now," and there wasn't a drama about it. So that's good; I'm happy I've learned to do that and trust that this was part of my process. I would go in my room and I wouldn't come out until I could feel the strength of my connection again – what I would call my normal waking consciousness.

It was kind of an organic thing; I didn't plan to do it this way. It was just out of desperation that I did this. I was in my room and, "Okay, what's up and down? What's what? I don't like this," and I'd just start in on myself. And pretty much nine out of ten times, it would start with me feeling like I needed to write a letter to Kalindi. I would start writing a letter, and I would have a mood of desperation in it.

Notes:

I would feel like I had to say something and bring something to her attention, or I had to know something. It was one of those two things, or both.

I would be thinking, "I've got to know something, because once I know it, then I can feel better." Or, "I've got to say it, because I've got to bring something to her attention, because the thing I want to bring to her attention is what is making me feel this way and then she can fix it." That description is simplifying what I went through in my room, but that is kind of the mood of it. And sometimes it was a letter to God that I wrote.

Sometime early on in this letter writing process, I recognized that it's not about writing a letter, it's about writing myself back to my connection, writing myself upward to my connection. My focus on the letter writing was helpful in that way, because then it was a tool to sort things out.

So that was the recurring thing that would happen. I had a lot of self-judgment that I was doing that, because I did not think that it was okay. On one hand, I had acceptance for it, but then on the other hand, the way I felt when it was going on was really bad. And I just couldn't make sense if it was okay or not. But I did it anyway, because that was the only way I knew to do.

I would get in the room and I was all churned up, and I would sit down at my desk, but almost automatically

Notes:

I just had to walk. I had to walk to match whatever was going on in my mind; I would just start pacing.

Now, this part is really interesting. I would get in a rhythm, some sort of rhythm of just talking and walking as if there was somebody there. The rhythm would be this: I would be walking and talking and I would be saying "Damn! Why do I feel this way? I hate it when this happens! How can we do this thing that she is asking? How can we do this? We can't do this. This is the seventeenth plan! Arunghhh!! Okay, so I will throw that one away and I will start on this one."

I would get in a rhythm where I was able to just start saying what was going on in the mind. Just like you are sitting there right now and you have stuff going on in your mind. All day we have stuff going on in our mind. But we never verbalize it. How much of what goes on in our mind do we ever actually verbalize? I could feel that if I wasn't verbalizing it, it would stay in there and it would have to come out, one way or another. It would have to go out the back door or the front door; and the back door would be that it would just disappear, but that didn't really happen. So the front door was me just walking and talking it out. I just had to get it out.

Me walking and talking dislodged the activity that was going on in the mind and transferred it out into words.

Notes:

_____

_____

_____

As soon as I could click into that, I could start to sort out fact from emotion, which were the two things going on. Sometimes it felt like separating truth from emotions. Sometimes it felt like facts, sometimes it felt like truth, but it was always separating emotions from the something else.

The funny thing is, when I could get the thoughts out of my mind, then I could hear the sound waves. It's like, my true self could hear better. Inside, it is just thought energy, it is just whatever thoughts are, whatever scientists could tell you a thought is. It was a strange thing, but when I dislodged it and got it out, I could hear more clearly and then I could see the situation more clearly.

I could hear myself talking; I would start to go into some case-building mode like, "No, I'm not going to do what I was asked to do, because this and that and the other thing and I'm not supposed to do that." And then I would start to hear, "Oh, that's emotion talking. Okay, that's emotion talking, so that is really not the place to go." So I could just increasingly move toward the truth; that is where I would go from there.

So I would be doing this talking and walking, and then I would get tired of doing that after an hour or so; so I would rewrite my letter. Let's say it would be a five-page letter, and because it would have overlays of emotion, fact, fiction, ideas, and fear in it, I would go back and I

Notes:

would take out one overlay. I would say, "I don't need to say that. That's not really what is going on. Let's push that aside. What is really the heart of the matter here? Okay, take that out." Then I would have three pages, then two, then one.

At some point I really knew that it wasn't about the letter. But I would still have to go through with it, even though I may have decided, "I'm not going to send this, but I still have to write it, because I'm in the middle of a process." And I would just keep doing this until I came to the natural conclusion that I didn't need to make the communication. I didn't need to know information. What I needed to do was *get back the connection*. I would feel, "That's it!" And I would feel myself righted again: mission accomplished.

Then I would come out of my room; sometimes it would be after an hour, sometimes it would be after three days. That was my thing, time and time again. Sometimes in the early days of the Mission it was very embarrassing and just awkward. Thank God the past is gone. Thank God it doesn't even exist anymore. The past is really gone. It doesn't even exist anymore. Kalindi finally came to peace with this process of mine. Maybe I could have put her at peace ten years ago by saying, "This is what I'm doing." But I didn't really know what I was doing. It

Notes:

was kind of a desperate action. And I would think, "I'm not supposed to be doing this. You are supposed to be on the floor releasing emotions." But there got to be a point on my path where I couldn't do that anymore. I remember feeling that I couldn't set aside time anymore to just scream or cry. It just felt unproductive. It felt like I was just going into something old.

I had to trust this other thing that I was doing. It was really fun after a while; I would get better and better at it. I would say "Ha, ha. Yes, that's just a bunch of crap." Then the conversation would be elevated each time, which was nice.

So to encapsulate what I learned: Through this process, each time I learned that whatever it was that I thought I needed to know or say was inconsequential to me feeling my normal connection to God. It was not relevant. It did not have anything to do with the deeper goal of feeling my connection to God. I would kind of have to relearn that lesson each time, because when you have something hit you, it's easy to be pulled away from feeling that connection.

Just because the spiritual work is not about issues doesn't mean issues are not going to come up. They are going to come up and come flying at you. The deeper you go, the trickier the issues get. I call them issues. I don't know what else to call them. You can call them blocks, things that

Notes:

130

come into your mind that cause a rift in your connection, a disturbance.

Each time I learned that logic, reasons, and convictions are not valid during the height of the intensity of emotions like that. I learned each time that holding out for an answer from Kalindi – or an expectation that she was going to help me with this – was the thing to let go of in order to feel my connection with God.

I discovered a couple of interesting things about the noise in my mind. When I am writing the letter it's still noise, but it is controlled, and I am trying to get the noise out. But when we make that noise in our mind, it dissipates focus on God. And you know what else it does? It compromises our ability to feel our desire. You can't be making the noise and feeling the desire it takes to make a connection. Those two things can't happen in the same moment. They are like oil and water; they are just not going to mix. So if you are making complaining noise like I'm describing, it's just keeping you distracted from the simple desire to be connected with God. I guess after all this time, I just noticed that my process of walking and talking and writing my letter was probably one way I was feeling my desire to get back to my connection with God. Maybe it doesn't look like my concept of what I would say desire was, but my intention was to get back to my connection.

Notes:

When you can't feel that desire, it makes things more unbearable; so you are heaping on a whole extra helping of suffering, rather than just dealing with it as quickly as you can.

When you don't feel that desire, you start feeling like a trapped victim.

On this Path, our first priority is the spiritual matter in our heart, not the material matter in our mind. That is the environment we live in, and like it or not, that is how it is. That is our way. *If the material concern causes a person to feel stuck, that concern has to yield to a higher spiritual matter; it has to yield to your connection.* The material concern has to yield.

What happens if you stay stuck in it? That moment of stuckness, that moment of holding on, is one thing that contaminates an environment of love. And we are desperately trying to always have an environment of love.

So when I am in my room like that, there is a struggle between light and dark going on. And there is nothing fundamentally wrong with that, because you always have the light and dark going on side by side. And you have to sort out, "Which is which? Which is which?"

A lot of times the darkness is the mind's attachment to cause, reason, and common sense. The darkness shows up as the mind's attachment to cause, reason, and common

Notes: _____

_____

_____

sense. So I am sitting down in my room and I am writing a lot of reason, a lot of common sense, a lot of logic, a lot of good idea, a lot of rationale; I am building an elevated case, but a case nonetheless, for why something should be different in order to make me feel better. This is what goes on in our minds. We want things to be different so that we will feel better.

Sometimes people have made courageous noises when they have felt they needed to stand strong for purity or some kind of change. But what I have learned is that even though there is something that maybe is helpful, the lion's share of what is spoken is just noise, because that person has forgotten their connection as their primary objective. It is their overall objective, because they are on the Path and we all know that – it is spoken, it is unspoken. We want to get rid of ego; we want to come into the light; we want more of God; we want more love; we want to let go of illusion. These are all things that are spoken and unspoken.

But when you are in the course of your daily affairs, pay attention to see if you are coming from a place of love or a place of fear. And I will tell you, everything traces back to one of those two things. *Fear is the driving force in this plane.* You've got love – real love, not sentimental love – or you've got some element of fear, even though you are some-times not going to relate it to fear or love: "Well, what does

Notes:

that have to do with this conversation?" This is just what I'm learning, so take it for what it's worth. Find it out for yourself if anything I'm saying about love and truth is true; but it's something to consider.

Another very humbling thing I learned was that I am susceptible to getting captured by illusion any time. It just happened in the last month. It was one of the times where it didn't go so well in my room. I went in my room. I tried to do my writing and talking process, but it was really a big one, and it was one that got away from me, and it went very fast. It was only a day, twenty-four hours. But in the end I thought, "Jeez, I just got side-swiped by the illusion, I think. Crap!"

But my overall score with my process was pretty good, and that's the thing: you want consistency. You want to get the consistent good score. But anybody is susceptible to being captured by the illusion at any time, so you have to find what reference point to truth and love you can find to get you out of it. For me, when the nature of my letter to Kalindi changes from one with a mood or tone of desperation to one where it's an offering of help, well, then I know I've crossed over into the light. I know I've made it that time. Instead of saying, "It shouldn't be this way," I can say, "It should be that way," or offer something constructive. That was my gauge.

Notes:

_____

_____

I learned that real surrender of separate will to God's will is something that just takes a lot of time. I'm still aware that I'm always in the process of surrender. I couldn't say where on a spectrum I am in terms of, "Getting on a path is here, and over here is ultimate enlightenment." I don't know where I am on that spectrum. How can I, because I don't even know what that spectrum is? But I do know that you cross a line where the nature of your surrender becomes different. I know there is a line, and I know surrender has to keep happening; and it changes.

Surrender is the objective and it is also the means. There is no ending point to it. There is an ending point to the ego, and I think that ultimate freedom means that ninety-nine percent of the ego is gone, and the one percent that is left has to do with the body and whatever you have to have just for walking-around purposes. Then the body dies and whatever ego was attached in that kind of way goes. In other words, you can't just let go of every single shred, because you have to walk around, and somehow there are aspects of ego that work for the functioning of the body. But that is not anything to be concerned about, because you know what ego there is to be concerned about.

Then, twenty years later, after starting this process of mine, I find this quote from Gourasana that just sort of spells out the whole thing I've been talking about:

Notes:

"If you do not have trust in God,
if you do not have faith in God,
*it means that you are in hell."**

You could sit there and chew on that for a lifetime. When I read it, I got it: "That is what has been going on with me." *Because to be separate from God means that you are in hell.* Here is how it was an actual experience of hell, not a concept of a fiery place. This is walking-around real-life stuff. Now some people are aware that they are in hell when they are in these states being stuck, of not having trust and faith. Some people are aware, and some people are covered over by the illusion when they are in these states, and they are not aware of the fact they are in hell.

"If you currently do not trust God, then you are in hell." What is "currently"? "Currently" is right now, however long this "now" moment lasts.

If you are driving in your car from point "a" to point "b," that is a "now" moment; and if during that moment you

* If you do not have trust in God, if you do not have faith in God, it means that you are in hell. Because to be separate from God means that you are in hell. Now some people are aware that they are in hell when they are in these states, and some people are covered by the illusion when they are in their states and they may not be aware of the fact that they are in hell. But if you currently do not trust God, if you currently do not have faith in God, then you are in hell, because you are separate from God.

And when you find yourself disconnected with God, not feeling the love, not feeling the power and the enthusiasm of being with God and doing His mission, it is because you are thinking about it and there is something you do not want to do. You are resisting doing what it is that you need to do. – *From the talk by Gourasana,* Trust and Faith, *available from www.miracle.org.*

Notes:

_____

_____

_____

currently don't have trust in God, if you currently do not have faith in God, then you are in hell. In that moment of driving a car, hammering a nail, eating lunch, showering, talking. Isn't that interesting? This is true. I know this is true. This is some of the nuts and bolts, I think, of the path and the journey Home. It is a very clear description of what goes on moment by moment in life.

You could, in theory – sometimes I like hypotheticals to illustrate a point – get to the end of a person's life and get some kind of spiritual record of what their life was like. You could say, "Yeah, you had six billion moments of this and ten billion moments of that. Now where do you go next?" We don't know what happens, but you could break it down technically, I suppose. Of course, the thing to do is be aware in the moment that it is a moment.

Gourasana goes on to say, *"And when you find yourself disconnected with God, not feeling the love …"* Now see, there is something. He is making a point about being disconnected from God. There is a sign: If I'm not feeling the love, then that has something to do with being disconnected. *"… not feeling the power…"* There is another clue. *"… not feeling the enthusiasm …"* There is another one. There are probably more. *"… not feeling the enthusiasm of being with God and doing His Mission, it is because you are thinking about it and there is something you do not want to do."* Well, there is

Notes:

me. That's the story I just told. Just figuring out what it is I don't want to do and then getting to the end of it and honestly thinking, "There isn't anything I have to do that I don't want to do. What the hell was that?" It was illusion. It was illusion and God playing out a dynamic, I guess you could say.

Gourasana's quote says, "You are resisting doing what it is that you need to do." That is what I was working on. "What am I resisting?" A lot of times I was just resisting acceptance of change. Change. I was resisting the flow.

You have got to pick the right world to live in. You have a choice. Some of you live in the right world; some of you don't. Some of you don't know that there are two worlds. I'm telling you, *there are two worlds*. One is the world in which you perceive yourself as the victim, and the other is the world in which you do not perceive yourself as the victim. Now there are shades of gray, of course; nothing is completely a hundred percent. But in actuality, this is what it comes down to. You are either more on one side or the other.

The trick is to not accept the premise – to reject the premise flat out – that you are in a world where you are a victim. You are in a world where most everything is not in your control. However, *every single shred of how you choose to perceive a situation is totally within your control*. Nobody forces you to perceive anything other than what you decide

Notes: Resisting acceptance of change
Resisting the flow

138

to perceive. That is a hell of a lesson. And *perception is king.* This is what I'm talking about after twenty years. Those of you who know me will understand why I say that I am the king of "no issues." I had thousands of issues, right and left, flying at me from everywhere, coming from my brain, coming from everywhere. I was awkward at times, and I didn't do things the way I should have, but I know in my gut that I had the perception that I always had choice. And even though I was struggling to make the right choice, the struggle was the opposite of holding on to an issue. When I was struggling, I could not hold on to it. I was endeavoring to just get it off of me.

You are going to have things come up that challenge your connection. For the sake of clarity, let's say that it is some kind of issue. Now let's say you take this issue, maybe in January, and you hold it and carry it, and you shut down or you get bewildered, or you lose your sense of center, and it has a mood of negativity, and you feel like you're being wronged, and you start sniffing blame in there. You take that with you through January, through February, on into the spring, summer rolls around, next thing you know it, the September Retreat is coming, and you still have that issue in September. And you get into sharing in a group, and you say something and some leader says, "That's an issue," and you say, "Oh, okay." But that's what it is.

Notes:

_____

_____

_____

The thing is not to hold the issue. An issue has a trigger, and how you choose to perceive the trigger determines whether it's going to turn into an issue or not. Certainly if you take the trigger and you say, "Shit! I can't go on with this! What, are they crazy?" Or, "I can't do this," or "That doesn't make any sense," then that would turn into an issue. I'm not speaking exclusively about your transformation; I'm talking about other areas of your life, like work, your family.

For example, I was standing there in Wal-Mart one day. We were there shopping. We were in the notebooks area; this guy was there and he wanted this particular notebook, and of course they didn't have it. They had nine thousand other things, but they didn't have the one thing that he wanted. And we were just looking for whatever we wanted, and I was just tuning in to the exchange he was having; he kept going on with the clerk, almost to the point of wanting to talk to the manager. Now here is this poor clerk. She doesn't have any decision-making ability on what the store carries on the shelf. She's just trying to help; she's being very nice. "I could get the manager if you want." She was really being really good. You could just feel how he was so constricted. "Wow, I wanted this here and I think you should have it here and I ..." on and on and on. You know what I mean.

Notes:

_____

_____

_____

Issues. You don't have to be happy about everything. You don't have to like everything. You don't have to like everybody. You're *not* going to like everything. You're *not* going to like everybody. You're going to have so many bad feelings come up, because this is a transformational path that forces the bad feelings to come up; because otherwise, what happens? The bad feelings are in there, and you go from year to year to year and you don't even know you have an issue going on.

It has taken so long to clarify this thing about issues; it drives me batty sometimes. I have to put it down, and I pick it up once a year and then put it down again. Because I get to where I think I've said everything there is to say about it. "What? Oh!" I get another request about something I have to do, and I go through another issue, and then I think that I have to make a talk about issues. "NO! I'm not going to make another talk about issues! Rrrr!!! I'm not going to make a talk about it. I'm going to get through this one, but we'll see if I'm going to make a talk about it."

Well, this is my talk about it. After all this time, this is my talk about it.

PATH OF LET GO, GIVE UP, SURRENDER

I *want to publish a book*
that has one page in it that says,
"Let go, give up,
and surrender to God."

People have a hard time grasping
what those words mean, but
you have to remember that it is
beyond the words.

But there's a part of you
that knows what that means:
TO LET GO
TO GIVE UP
TO SURRENDER TO GOD.

GOURASANA

Get Out
Of Your Mind

Spoken on June 11, 2008

The transformation that I am guiding you through is not a transformation of the mind. When I say that, I'm not talking about *not thinking* in your transformation – because this is a transformation of great thought. There is a very high level of thinking done with the Modern-Day Meditation, the GMP. In practicing the GMP, we think at a very high level. I'm not talking about that; I am talking about the mind in all of its chatter about everything.

Your mind starts thinking and running everything past you in your mind, saying, "You did that wrong, and you did this wrong, and maybe you did that right. Oh, what is this that I'm thinking about now? Maybe I have a feeling about this? Maybe I should go into the feeling about this?" Everything that comes across your mind could turn into a feeling or an issue, because you go inside and think that you have to work on those things or figure them out.

There are endless scenarios that can go on in the mind. And when you're done figuring out or letting things

Notes:

come into your mind from this lifetime, then things will start coming from your previous lifetimes. It's endless. You cannot do anything about all of that stuff. It's just stuff. Maybe it is stuff that happened to you, maybe it's not. Maybe it is new things that you are thinking about.

You are not meant to go into that area of your mind and solve everything that is coming up day after day. I want you to have very, very, very fast movement. Fast. And if you start thinking too much, it will slow you down. That is why I want you out of your mind and out of thinking about every little thing that crosses your mind.

You need to develop awareness. As you have heard before from various spiritual masters or teachers, you need to start to look at your mind and see what it is doing. It is just having a chatter box with itself. You need to just let it chatter away. Just look at it like you are watching TV and just let the film run. It could run forever. It doesn't mean anything. Let it run until something comes that, "Oh, I need to remember this." When that happens, you need to write it down on your RE* pad. Or if some feeling comes up and it causes your emotional body to be feeling right away, maybe you have to start crying because something happened to you or something

* Kalindi is referring to a pad of forms called "REmember"– for jotting down brief notes of one or two lines when you think of something you need to remember. This helps to keep your mind empty and your emotions calm.

Notes:

_____

_____

_____

is blocked that needs to move. In that case, the thing to do is to release the feeling. But most of the thoughts that come through your mind are just something to watch, like television.

Don't look for the cause of your emotional blocks unless you are specifically going in search of that due to blocked emotions and feeling stuck. If this is the case, you need to do the GMP at that point and practice *all* of the parts of that meditation. In that case, specifically go within to find out what it is that is going on with you. That is a different endeavor than letting your mind constantly run thinking this, thinking that, "Does she love me? Does she not? I wonder about this, I wonder about that. I wonder this, I wonder that." It all goes on and on and on and on until you become a yogi and have the ability to just shut it off. You don't have that yet, but you can take the perspective of watching your mind chatter like you are watching a film every day. Your mind chatter is like a constant film running, and you are watching it. Just write something down if something comes up that you need to remember.

Don't work on the stuff in your mind. Work on stuff in meditation *after* you have gone deep and have connected to God. Don't take all of the stuff in the mind into your meditation. Throw out that stuff at the beginning of your meditation, and then meditate with God.

Notes:

_____

_____

_____

My teachings have never been about the mind and figuring everything out. What is going on in the mind is all based on fear. Fear runs the mind.

What you really need to do when you need to solve something is to do what Gourasana says: "The only solution to the problem is to go deeper." If you just go a little deeper, you will see that your mind cannot follow you. So in your daily life, if you can situate yourself just a little bit deeper, you will see that part of your mind doesn't live there. Then if you go a little bit deeper, you will be in what I call "a daily meditative state." That is a meditation for the marketplace, a "marketplace meditation." That is where you can walk around in your meditative state connected all throughout the day. If you do that, you won't have this mind crap completely stopping you. *Be with God.* And then when you are in meditation, you can go all the way deep. As you come closer and closer to God, you will learn how to be with Him completely in union and how to be in this world.

I want you to just drop out of your head and come deeper within; focus on the place inside beneath your chest. Focus there, come there, stay there.

It is important that you listen to my direction here. It is important that you do not get stuck in your mind, if you want to get free. This path is not about letting the mind go all over the place. I am teaching the straight and narrow path to the love of God, to Home, for those that want Home. And that path is not about the mind. And it is important, for those that need it, to learn how to get out of your mind, unhook the mind, and fall deeper into God.

Notes:

_____

_____

_____

Rapid Speed Transformation

Spoken on October 18, 2006

I have said this path of transformation is "rapid-speed transformation." What that means is that the energy of God that is coming in at this time, is specifically pushing people to move forward materially and spiritually at a very rapid speed. People can evolve to a level of consciousness in this one lifetime that may have taken them perhaps sixty lifetimes or more to achieve without the special assistance from God that is helping at this time.

This energy from God that is coming in is not just coming to Miracle of Love. It is pushing in to the whole world; the whole world is feeling pressed, and they don't know why. He is pressing in all over the place, and people don't know what's happening to them.

The speed of this transformation is what makes the transformation so difficult. This is why there is so much "floor work"* to do in meditation. The meditation used in this transformation is called the "Meditation for This Age"

---

* See "Modern-Day Meditation" in Definition of Names and Terms in the back of the book.

Notes:

because the speed of transformation is so rapid during this day and age. And this meditation was brought in specifically for this rapid transformation.

As I have said in the past, it is necessary to reach a certain velocity to actually break the hold the illusion has on you, if you want to break the cycle of birth and death in this lifetime*.

Human beings just don't normally move forward that fast spiritually or materially. They don't change their lives every single day. They don't normally change their minds and consciousness every single day of their life. That is what the transformational energy of the Heavenly Host is pushing people to do. And if you connect to this energy, it will push you. Sometimes you will just have to scream in order to respond to the feeling of being pushed.

In transformation, people are praying, "Please, please, Lord, please take me and take me fast," because they can feel the Lord, and they want to go fast enough so that they can make it out of this illusion in this lifetime. The Lord with the Host has come to facilitate just that.

You are asking for it to be fast transformation, and the Lord is fulfilling that desire. It doesn't feel good simply because it is hardly possible for the human mind to travel at

---

* See the talk, *Take-off Velocity*, in Kalindi's *Bottom Line Series*, for this explanation.

Notes:

that speed. It is hardly possible to change and be open and go that fast, for the nervous system to move that fast.

In transformation, many things need to change that you just don't normally change in a lifetime. You are changing beliefs, deep-seated beliefs, because you are going so fast that you come to realize complete opposite beliefs than what you believed before. That happens to you maybe every month: You come to a completely different realization, and that realization changes your whole life. Then you have to change so many things in your life because of that new realization.

It is important to let go of the issues, because nothing that you are going through is really about any issue. If you start thinking about issues, you get stuck in your mind and stop along the way. While you are going so fast, you start thinking, "Why do I feel this way? What is this about?" You start making your spiritual movement be about issues when the reality is you are just going so fast. You just need to scream and let go and just keep going and not get so hung up on what you think you are feeling, because what you think really doesn't have anything to do with how fast you are transforming. He is just pushing you and pushing you and pushing you, because you asked and prayed, "Take me fast." He is pushing you faster than you can comprehend. It is so important that you use the meditation practice to help facilitate the rapid changes you are going through.

Notes:
_____

_____
_____

Given the speed you are dealing with, have some compassion for yourself, for what you are actually doing and for what you have said "yes" to. Have compassion for each other, that we are in this transformation together; we are doing it for God and for the ultimate benefit of humankind.

In this talk series, I gave a talk about pushing through the walls when they come up and not really worrying what the walls are; just push them down and come into the light. What the walls are – that you are pushing down – are unconsciousness; they are walls of unconsciousness that would have taken you many, many lifetimes to get through. You are pushing through unconsciousness, not just from this lifetime.

You are trying to gain consciousness so that you can awaken into 100 percent light. You are trying to do it in this lifetime, and the Host and Gourasana are here to help you to make it in this lifetime. They are here to push you and pull you fast enough so that you can make it. This is another reason why it is so important to get out of the issue work and let go into Him. Just understand: "He is pushing me and I'm just letting go. I'm just going to get on the floor and scream and cry and let go." Or "I'm just going to let go through my awareness." Or "I am just going to understand that this is a hard day today. He's just pushing in on me and I'm just getting through today. By the power of choice I'm

Notes:

just changing my mind; I'm just going to have a positive outlook on everything and just understand that I'm traveling very, very fast spiritually. I'm not going to forget that for one second. I'm in His hands. He's pushing me. I asked for it. I'm helping with His Mission. I've got to go fast. And I've got to just endure whatever I have to endure."

Want to surrender to the push. Want to have it. Want to surrender to it, and be grateful that you found Him. Don't resist it. There is no time to resist it. Really, there is no time to resist it. That just doubles the trouble. It just makes it so much harder. Be grateful that you are going so fast.

Notes:

_____

_____

_____

In the Gateway

Conversation Between Kalindi and a Disciple

Spoken on July 14, 2006

Kalindi addressing a disciple: I want to talk to you about what has been going on with you and your realizations since we started this conversation about letting go and gathering all your attention and focus, focusing on Gourasana, and just going. I know some things have been happening to you.

Disciple: The biggest thing I noticed is the feeling of internal movement. That has been undeniable and alive inside of me. It actually is very difficult to even try to put words to it, because it's just there. The difference between this feeling of movement and how I have been living my path for years is like day and night, because the movement has a feeling of aliveness and energy to it, like literally something moving inside, where much of my path, it almost felt dead inside me. My mind was engaged in "Okay, what do I need to let go of? What do I need to do next? What do I have to do in order to let go of the next thing? What do I still need to break free?" and constantly looking. But the distinction right now is between the feeling of aliveness, the internal

Notes:

154

movement that is just moving forward, and the feeling of deadness. And I was thinking, "Does that mean all of these years that I was feeling dead, I wasn't moving?" I can't believe that that is true.

Kalindi: No, that is not true, because the process you have been going through has been freeing you from all kinds of illusion. Without that, you wouldn't have been able to just step into this clear focus and gather all of your attention and just go to God. Like I have been trying to tell all of you, all this time, "Just come. Just let go and just come." But you couldn't in the past. You were hanging on to so many illusions. When you first started the work, your two hands were tightly grasping on to the illusion. Now He can just take you. You can gather all of your focus. You even know what that feels like. You can do that, whereas before, so many illusions were just pulling you in every direction. Now so many people are ready with all ten fingers up.

Transformation can be speeded up a lot now for the people that are coming to Miracle of Love. People can know that that movement is where they want to get to; they can understand it as well as they can. In each workshop they can be reminded that "This workshop is just prying you free from all the illusions that are keeping you from this, because this is what you really have to do: You have to get to the point where you will just move. Just focus all of your

Notes:
_____
_____
_____

attention, gather all of your energy, and focus it toward Gourasana." (That is from a quote in *Breaking the Cycle of Birth and Death*.*) Then your movement will just internalize, and you will just move. There won't be a moment that you are just not moving, and moving, and moving. You can't even stop to figure out what you are moving through, because it is going so fast. That is the rapid-speed transformation that Gourasana is talking about, where He is just going to take you. He promised this, but you have to do all of your work to get there. You have to get to the point where you can gather all of your focus and all of your attention toward Him, and you have let go of everything so there is nothing in the way, so He can just take you.

What did you say to me about that tunnel feeling, and the meteors?

Disciple: Well, the internal movement has the feeling of being inside a tunnel, going straight toward Gourasana at such a speed that whatever illusion is going on inside of me that needs to be let go of, it is just like crashing off of me. The movement is so fast that I'm not even able to try to grab on to "What is that illusion I am supposed to let go of?" Some illusion is there – it moves; another illusion is there – it

---

* *"Listen to this carefully. If you can gather all of your energy, all of your consciousness and direct it toward Me, then I can very easily take you into My arms, and you will be Home. I am awaiting your arrival. When will you come?"* Quote #24, Gourasana, *Breaking the Cycle of Birth and Death*, Miracle of Love, 4th Edition, 2007

Notes:

moves. You said the other day, "Yeah, once in a while a meteorite [an illusion] might hit you in the head. You feel it and you have to cry, and then you get up and you keep moving." But the feeling of being "focused" is almost like having blinders on, just going straight in one direction.

What is surprising me is that I am able to function fine in the material world. I think I had the idea that to have this kind of movement, you had to be on the floor in meditation or in a Gateway meditation. I could not even conceive that this could be happening while you are just living your life, although I feel this is the energy you, The Lady, and the Core are living in. I feel you all living in this energy. It is identifiable. It is palpable. It didn't occur to me that I could live in that energy. I thought this kind of energy and movement could only happen on the floor in meditation.

I also realized that I had some fear that this movement is going to stop. And so if it stops, then I gather all my focus: I know there is some illusion that got me; I don't need to figure out what it is. I gather my focus, and I turn toward Him. I am still thinking, "Okay, that means I have to beg Him."

Kalindi: No, you do not want to beg Him. You just want to stay calm; control your being. Don't get flipped out. Just turn your focus again toward Him within. Go within, pray, and turn your focus toward Him. You may sit down

Notes:
_____

_____

_____

for two hours and put church music on and turn your focus within, toward Him. Pray, "Gourasana, please, take me, and please help me stay focused on You, only You." Then you have to stay in that focus. At a certain point, that energy will take you over and you will not be able to get out of that focus. And if you ever feel yourself out of it, all you have to do is turn your focus there, and it's right there; He is right there.

Disciple: That is what I feel with the Core.

Kalindi: Yes, they are living in that energy, and that is union with God. That will just keep taking you and taking you until you are just filled by Him, and His energy just takes you, and takes you, and takes you. He will answer your prayer, and He will just keep coming, and coming, and coming, and coming.

Once you finally find this flow, it is the most precious thing to find, because it is Him, and you are with Him finally. You just keep walking toward Him and keep going, and then when something gets to be too much – which it might, because He might bump up against an illusion and then He can't come in more. He is just pushing on you, and you are pushing forward, and there just comes a feeling like there is a big rock there. That is when there is a feeling of intensity building, and that is when you have to get on the floor and scream. When you are on the floor screaming, the energy starts moving through you and the energy moves that block;

Notes:

the energy moves through you and just crashes through that illusion. Then after a while, you just get up and you are just moving again with Him. Sometimes you are on the floor because you are feeling Him so much you just have to cry in the love of God that you feel. But when you get to this place, you no longer need to be on the floor for two or three hours crying for God; you only need to get on the floor and cry if there is a block that is so big that you just have to cry and cry it away.

That is where I have been trying to guide you all, and it worked. Whatever we did, it worked, because it is only about fourteen years of transformation on this path for most of you, some of you ten years. And in ten years, to have gotten a whole group of people to where they are walking with Him, and He is just taking them, that isn't very long.

He is just opening this door now to all of you, because now you are ready to come. We have to tell people to get it very clear what they are doing. The workshops and seminars help to free you from all of the illusions. That needs to happen so you can get to this internal movement, where your focus is gathered on Him and in Him; so you can get to the point of "Here I am, Lord, with two hands up, all fingers open, coming to You; take me." People are praying that prayer all the time while they are doing this work of prying free, and they need to pray that. But they are praying it so

Notes:

_____

_____

that they can get to this place where you are, where internalized fast movement is happening. There is nothing externalized; there is really nobody to talk to about any of your problems anymore. It is just between you and Him. And you might come up against a rough spot here and there, and you can talk to your buddy, but you know that it is just going to be up to you. You just have to get on the floor when you are just not moving. But isn't the internal movement fast?

Disciple: Unbelievably fast.

Kalindi: Every day you are changing; you wake up and you are different every single day?

Disciple: Completely. And this all started from witnessing you letting go. You were dealing with something, and in the next moment you just had let go. I could see it in your face, and you said, "Ah, I just let go." Then we talked about it, and all this movement for me started with the realization that you do not need to know what you are letting go of. All of these years, I have been looking, "What is the next thing I need to let go of?" And then I focused on that, and that thing just became this big issue I needed to let go of. Now, with this movement, it is like Gourasana has just been pulling me through this tunnel.

Kalindi: Once you knew that you did not have to know what you were letting go of, you could let Gourasana just take you?

Notes:

_____

_____

_____

Disciple: Yes. It freed my mind to realize you don't have to know what you are letting go of. You have told me for years, "Let go of your mind, let go of your mind, let go of your mind." I have been working on letting go of my mind. But, it let go. Something let go. And that is why I think I am so surprised. That is what it feels like, just one surprise after another. My mind feels more able, and clearer. Now my spiritual work feels different.

Kalindi: And it is very internalized. See, the people need to know that this is where they are headed. But if we say that, I don't know if the people, coming with all of their illusion, can straight off the bat just come and do this.

Disciple: If it's even possible?

Kalindi: I do not know if it is possible without all the workshops and seminars and looking at your illusions and working through a big chunk of them. I do not know if it is possible to even understand or hear. But they can try. They can keep trying: "I am just going to let go." They can try. At least that door needs to be open to them, and we need to teach that. But I always thought I was teaching that.

Disciple: You were teaching that. About 13 or 14 years ago, you were with a group of us – there were maybe 80 of us in a circle – and you just said, "Okay, who is going to let go now?" in the same way that you are talking about it now. From where I was spiritually then, I thought, "I will!

Notes:
_____

_____

161

I am going to let go. I will let go right now."And you said,
"No, I mean, like really let go." I didn't have any idea what
you were talking about. What I am experiencing now is
what you were talking about, but I had no idea. I just did
the best I could with whatever understanding I had at the
time with my mind, and whatever connection I had from
The Intensive.

Kalindi: God had to keep prying your fingers loose one by
one from the illusion, prying your mind loose so you can get
to where you are now.

Disciple: You have always been saying it. It is not like you
have not said it. I remember that so distinctly, and thinking,
"Wait a minute, I am letting go. Don't tell me I am not letting
go. I am letting go. I want to. I am going."

Kalindi: You all have been working so hard on the path,
and that is why you can never give up, because now you are
there, and now you are coming Home. Now you just have to
constantly give full attention and focus and never lose your
way out of here.

Now you are in the Gateway, and now you are just
walking Home. It is at a very rapid clip, because you are
going to be Home way before you leave this world, and you
are going to take a lot of people with you. How can you not
turn around and take people with you once you are there?
You are now on the phone calling anybody that you can talk

Notes:

to and trying to tell them, "Come, do the path this way," using every type of words that you can try to tell them how you are finding your way now. The people are listening and they want to come.

Disciple: I was talking to another disciple this morning, and he said something about finding his next thing to work on, and I said, "No, you don't have to do that. You just notice the illusion, and you just let go of that thing." But I was thinking it's not even the words that I speak to him, that will get across to him; it is the energy of the words that is going to impact him. I know he could feel that energy. Somehow the energy itself communicates; the energy gets communicated to the person and leaves that person ignited to just "Okay, I don't know what it is, or how I am going to do it, but I am going where that energy is," because that is what you want. When I was with The Lady all those years I would say, "In my toughest times, I do not care, because I want what she has. I want that energy and movement."

Kalindi: All of you that keep going in your transformation are going to be examples for all the people that are now coming to the path. They are going to say, "I don't know how, but I want that, what those people have."

Disciple: It's like a miracle.

Kalindi: I am very happy for you.

Disciple: Thank you so much, Kalindi, for never giving up

Notes:

on us. I cannot imagine how frustrating it was for you, all these years of feeling everyone's sincerity and desire and doing everything you possibly could to move us spiritually and tell us how to move along the path. So thank you.

Kalindi: Thank Gourasana.

Disciple: Thank you, Gourasana, and The Lady, and the Core, really.

Kalindi: Thank David Swanson. Thank God there is a way out of here.

But now, it is going to be so interesting to you in your path and what goes on, because it is a whole world inside of you that you are going to start going through as you leave this plane of illusion and enter into the true realm, because that is where you are walking into, is Home. You are going to walk straight out of the illusion into the true realm. So everything of this world is going to drop off of you while you are still in this world, while you are still functioning. You are going to go through a lot of changes, and you are going to do it inwardly; you are going to know what to do. You are going to change. It is going to become richer. You are going to become deeper. Your awareness is going to expand on its own. Your consciousness is just going to grow and grow. Your realizations are just going to come. When I talk, when The Lady talks, when Jim talks, you are going to hear it from a whole other place. If you go back and listen to all of

Notes:

_____

_____

_____

Gourasana's talks and my talks, it is going to be like a whole new thing that you have never heard before. Because when you listened to it before, you were listening to it from the place of a struggling seeker, and now you can listen to it from an open place, where "Yeah, that is right, that is right. I have never heard that, but that is exactly right." You have so much, and now you just keep going.

Disciple: Thank you.

Don't Stop at the Most Crucial Time

Excerpts from:
"Letting Go, The Real Path," spoken on July 12th, 2006 and
"Precious Truth Not to Be Lost," spoken on July 13th, 2006

On the path straight Home, everyone has to get to the point where they let go, give up, and surrender. Once they embark on that journey, God just starts to take them.

Once someone starts doing the advanced work, they have already surrendered to God to a great degree. They have already surrendered and already know "I am giving my life to God. I fully know that I am saying, 'Yes, I want to surrender.' I am letting go, giving up, surrendering. And I know what that means." Once you embark upon that journey of letting go, giving up, and surrendering, God really starts to just take you.

At that point, you have to stop trying to have a say-so in how you want your transformation or life to be, and you just have to tolerate what you have to go through in your spiritual transformation.

There is no bargaining. It is God's way. That is the only way. People are stopping their transformation at a crit-

Notes:

ical point, and it is all turning into issues and fears and doubts and wasting precious time, which means that maybe they won't make it Home in this lifetime. You can get hung up on an issue for years and years and years, and you find yourself a comfortable niche within your spiritual life and you never will cross through it. That will stop you from making it Home.

If you want to make it Home in this lifetime, don't talk about any issues about anything, because you have no time to waste.

You need to know that when it gets to the point where you feel that you are at the end of your rope, and what you are going through and feeling is too much to tolerate, it is because God is closing in on your illusion and starting to tear it out of you. *That is the exact point when you just have to get on the floor and scream.* At that point, you have to go to the depth where you are crying from your guts. You have to go to the point that you think you are just going to choke because you are crying so deeply. You have to keep going until the energy stops, and then you will have just let go of something. At some point the feeling of intensity calms down, and you are just lying there and God is just soothing you. When it is all over, you can somehow get up and go on. There is still more to let go of, but you can go on, and you know that you can make it through another day.

Notes:

_____

_____

_____

For a couple of years, your transformation will be like that. Everyone still has some of this to do, even those who have done the advanced work. Some people who have gone through years of transformation are practically free from illusion, and they have walked their path in a long-drawn-out way. But there is still this one part of them that just hasn't done this part of the path; it is the part that is still questioning.

You stop when it gets to the point where it is really hard, and you don't know what's going on or what to do. You start to wonder, "What is this that I am feeling? What is this fear, and what is this?" At that point you start to analyze, "What is this that I am feeling? What can I do about this?" When you get into that questioning, you turn it into an issue or you try to psychoanalyze, "What is happening to me?" That is the point that you are stopping the precious movement where the Lord is taking you into that place where it is unbearable, where you just have to face it. You are in the corner where you have nowhere to move but to Him, and you squeeze your way through it. You just scream your way through.

People keep coming up against the point where they are supposed to just hit the meditation floor and go to God, but instead they go into questioning when they hit up against something inside of themselves. They start to analyze what they are feeling: "What is this? What am I feeling? I don't know if I want to feel this. And what is this? What am I afraid of?" They even take it into workshops. They keep going in the direction of trying to figure it out instead of just letting it get so acute, with no way out. They steer off of the path of let go, give up, surrender. At this point, they just have to get on the floor and just start screaming, because there is no bargaining with God. There is no "Wait a minute."

People get so much light from going through workshops and events on the path. They dump so much baggage in those events, so they feel so much ecstasy. People just can't wait to get back in the workshops so they can get more light, and then get more ecstasy; "Wow, this was the best workshop ever." But they are still not going fast enough for their freedom. They have got to get to the fast path of let go, give up, and surrender.

We have the workshops because a lot of people are going to have to travel bit by bit by bit. Gourasana said He is going to pry people's fingers loose, finger by finger. That is what the workshops are doing. Each workshop is prying one finger free. That is one way to move spiritually. The other way to move is to let go, give up, and surrender, especially when it comes to people doing the advanced work. Let go, give up, surrender is the way. No more prying each finger free, finger by finger. It is about movement now, fast movement.

Notes:

Once people are doing the advanced spiritual work, they have made the decision to surrender to God. It doesn't matter anymore what they think about this or think about that. God doesn't care about making a deal with you. He doesn't care how you feel about this or how you feel about that. The idea is you just go, and when it gets to feeling bad, then you are just on that floor screaming in meditation. Do not walk the path taking "exits," ways to avoid getting on the floor in meditation, ways of analyzing what you are feeling and figuring out why you aren't surrendering.

When it gets to be excruciating and your ego is just being squeezed to death, you just have to get on the floor and scream. That is different from when you started your spiritual work, when you were on the floor praying and crying and trying to release everything. That is what people on the Path have been doing in meditation all these years. They have been just praying and grueling it out on the floor, putting their effort toward prayer, and trying to get to God.

What I am talking about now for those who are doing the advanced work is different. You just get taken and ripped through whatever of the rest of the ego is left. When it feels too bad, you don't stop and try to figure it out – or try to figure out if you want to go with God or not. You go. That means you "hit the floor"* and you scream through what-

---

* See "Modern-Day Meditation" in Definition of Names and Terms in the back of the book.

Notes:

ever it is and then the energy comes. You just go with God until the energy stops. Then you stand up and go to the next level. You keep going. You don't stop, ever. When the energy comes, you scream, even when you want to stop.

God is here to help you and will help you one way or another, because this Incarnation has come to give help individually to each seeker. But you have to let go. Then He can help you pry your fingers loose from the illusions you are hanging on to. Out of His mercy and love, He has come here with special assistance and energy that will help you. God is so anxious to help the suffering souls; He is ready to help each and every individual get free from the illusions that are binding them. Gourasana has said that God will assist people to pry each finger free that is gripping on to the illusion, if that is what it will take.

Some of you are stuck wallowing in issues, but it is not only issues you are stuck in. You are stopping right when you can make it through a big letting go of something in your transformation. You are stopping right when it is an opportunity of "Ah, now I can go." You get so scared, or your ego comes up, or you begin questioning, or something happens, and instead of going to the floor, you stop. That is right at the point where you could go to God. For some of you, you may need to have somebody there, like a spiritual leader, that can help push you through.

Notes:

_____

_____

_____

Issues have nothing to do with surrendering to God. Issues have everything to do with you hanging on. You talking about your issues, is you talking about everything that you just want to think about. You are just doing personal growth work when you are in issues. This path is beyond personal growth. This is about letting go of everything. Did you know you said "yes" to God? That means unconditional "yes." You already willingly gave away your preference as to whether you are going to have it your way. If you get freaked out, get on the floor and scream. If you are sitting there and you think your head is going to burst open – you can't take it – then get on the floor and scream. Pray to Gourasana, because He is going to come and get you. This is what it feels like to let go.

When people are sitting in front of a spiritual leader, they want to sit there and have the leader talk to them, and talk to them, and talk to them about what they are going through spiritually. They want the leader to pacify them so they walk out of the room and feel better. People want someone to talk to them when they are freaked out. This is so they never have to let go. They talk to someone, and then they feel better. Then they just start living their lives again, and when something comes up that freaks them out, they go talk to somebody again until they feel better. They never hit that peak point where they have to let go and Gourasana comes

Notes:

and picks them up. They never hit that point where they have to surrender, where they are just hanging on a string and just praying to God, "I hope You are there, because I have nothing to hang on to." You have to hit that place so many times on your spiritual path.

That is the path of let go, give up, surrender. All of the other work, all of the workshops, are fine, because they are prying everybody's fingers free, like Gourasana said that this special assistance from God will do: God is going to just pry everybody's fingers loose. It is like everyone's fists are tightly closed, and He is just going to pry them loose one finger at a time. While He is trying to get one finger loose, everybody is fighting to keep that finger down. But God is going to get the fingers loose.

Once you say "yes" to God, once you really say "yes" to Him, once you say, "I give you my life," then your job is to tolerate the transformation and stop stopping. When your transformation gets unbearable, when you feel like you are in a tight squeeze and there is no way out, the place to go is into that unbearable feeling. Go into it until it gets so bad that there is no place to go but to get on the floor and start screaming, going to your depth, and just going deeper into Him and praying to Him and waiting it out until it lifts.

That is the transformation that takes you Home. Transformation where you keep stopping and starting and

Notes:

analyzing everything that is happening won't take you Home. The transformation I know is where you just keep going toward Him, and you just keep letting it get to the point where it is just so unbearable that you have to get on the floor and scream. In that moment, you are breaking through to the other side. And He is right there to help you. Go through the fear. Go through whatever it was that brought you to that point and just go through it with Gourasana, and stop the questioning, "What is it? What's happening? I feel fear. What is that fear?" Stop asking, "What is that fear?" and just face it and go through it. Let it get so bad that you are trembling and you have to get on the floor. Don't get on the floor and pray, and pray, and pray for something to happen. Rather, let it happen. Let Him get you. Let Him take you over. Let Him take you into a corner where you have no place to run, no one to ask anything about. No one can do anything about it anymore, because the Lord is just taking you.

With Gourasana, the path of "Let go – just do it. Don't analyze it all – just go" is possible. He is prying your fingers away from the illusion, and you are getting freer and freer. Then you come to the point where you can hear the stark reality of surrender. And that is the end of it all. That is scary to hear in the very beginning of transformation, so you let go finger by finger, not all at once. But you are faced

Notes:

with surrender at the time of death. There is nowhere to go; there is no one to help you. And if you haven't let go of the illusion before that, it's too late.

There is nowhere else to go now. You have let go so much. And now there is one thing to do, and that is turn your focus to the Lord. It is not even enough to just turn to the Lord. You have to turn to the One that has come to take you Home. I am saying Lord Gourasana has come to take you Home. There is a special assistance and special energy available; you have to turn to the Host, and turn to Lord Gourasana to connect to that assistance.

That specifically is where you have to go. You need to focus yourself into that energy. Gourasana said, "If you can turn all of your energy, gather all of your focus, and turn it toward Me, than I can easily take you from this plane of illusion." He promised to take people Home. He is the one that made the promise. He is standing right there with the same promise; so when are you going to turn to Him?

No one is going to do it on their own. I am here as His Voice, and I have to tell you, you have to go to Him. You know all along the way, it is okay, you can pray to God in whatever way you want; but when you want to go through the Gateway, He is the one standing in the Gateway ready to just pluck you out of the illusion. This final turning your focus to Him and just praying, "Okay, I am just ready,

Notes:

_____

_____

_____

please take me," and just facing it and going through it, is what needs to happen. That needs to be done with Gourasana helping. So there are two things going on: focus on Him and praying to Him to help you move through the illusion into Him.

You have to pull Gourasana to you. Pull Him to you. Ask, "Please, Gourasana, take me now; I am ready. I give You full permission. I know You are the way out of here." You have to have trust and faith. Those of you who have been doing this work for some time have already connected so deeply to Him and His energy. You are not blindly going toward Him. You already have such a deep connection to Him. You are connected to His energy. If you don't go toward it, you can't finish up your transformation. You can't get out. Gourasana is the one that has made the way out. He is the one that is going to pull you through when you face those times where you are just up against the corner.

Notes:
_____

_____

_____

When Will You Start in Earnest?

Spoken on August 19, 2007

I have one thing to say to everyone, and that is, don't sit around and wait for something to happen in your spiritual transformation. Don't sit around complaining and wallowing, thinking that transformation is too hard.

You are praying to God to "Take me, break me, smash my ego." When the answer comes and your ego is getting smashed, don't complain about how you don't want that to happen and you don't like how it feels when it happens. Don't try to put everything back together. Rather, get on the floor and cry and scream and let go.

When the smash or the rip of the ego comes, say, "Thank you very much, and please, I want to go faster." Stand up on your feet and be strong, for it is the strong that will make it. Be strong and pray to God for more strength. *Pray for more strength.*

Get going with the Heavenly Host, with Gourasana who has come to help you with this. He will do His part.

Notes:

177

Will you let go of the many things that must be let go of? When will you start? *When will you start in earnest?* There are so many things that need to be let go of. There are things inside of you that comprise the basic structure of the being of illusion that you don't even know about yet. You don't have any time to waste if you are going to make it Home.

If your spiritual goal is to get freer and freer, you are doing just fine at whatever rate you're going. You are doing fine. What I am speaking here is for the people that have the desire to go Home in this lifetime, for the people with the desire to become enlightened, for the people who want self realization. You cannot sit around and think anybody is going to do it for you. It is so possible to break free of the material illusion, but it takes everything to make it.

There are some people that are approaching a state of full awareness, and they are approaching Home. There are those that have already achieved their heart's desire, union with the Lord. They are still constantly letting go, just as I am also constantly letting go and will be for the rest of my life.

Notes:

The Lord Resides Deep in Your Heart

Spoken on July 20, 2006

If you want to break free, if you want to move through the illusion that has you bound, if you want to move through it at a rapid rate fast enough to break you free, if you want God to help you move quickly, *you must go within, you must stay focused, and you must stay deep!* You must learn how to stay deep and how to stay focused within and not lose that focus within. As you stay focused in that depth, you will automatically stay in a prayerful state.

This is something that you need to endeavor to achieve. As you situate yourself in that state and don't come out of it, just focus and stay in your prayer and your depth; then the illusion has no way to be in that depth with you.

The illusion cannot be in that depth with you when you are situated in your depth with God and prayer. The illusion doesn't fit in there; it has to let go! As you focus more and more with the Lord, the illusion begins to fall away. The more you stay focused and in your depth and prayer, the more the illusion starts to fall away: more, and more, and

Notes:

179

more. It will continue to fall away more and more as you stay within with the Lord in your prayer and in your depth. You will just move, and you will be in a let-go state, and this illusion will continue to fall away.

You may or may not even know what it is that is falling away. You will just keep changing. When you need to know what an illusion is that you come up against, you will ask, "What is it that I can do to move through this illusion?" You will get the answer, and then you will do what it is that is told to you within in order to move through that illusion. Then you move through that illusion, and you stay focused in your depth. Usually, you have a breakthrough, and then you see, "Oh, there is the light at the end of the tunnel"; you feel your true being, and you feel you can breathe. There is a great connection and a great joy, because more of your self has come into being. Having more of your connection and more of your self means more self realization has happened: more of your true being is present.

Then go back deep within in prayer, and stay focused. Just stay focused in prayer and keep going. Keep moving and going, and the illusion falls away. The illusion cannot be there when you are in that single-pointed focus. It just falls away as you single-mindedly move forward like an arrow piercing, just moving, moving, moving. The illusion is then just flying away, flying away, flying away. God is just taking

Notes:

_____

_____

_____

you. Why? Because you *only* want Him, and you are focused on *only* Him. You remain in your depth and you stay in your depth. Why? Because you *only* want Him. You are not interested in this material world. You *only* want the Lord, so you stay in your depth, and you stay in your prayer, and you stay focused, and you pray, "Lord, please take me deeper." And you stay in that focus.

The reason you come out of that focus is because you want to be in material consciousness. You want something to satisfy you. You want to go to the movies. You want to go take a break. You want to go have some fun. But when you are ready to come Home, you *must* gather all of your attention and all of your focus and turn within to the Lord in your depth and move toward Him. He will then quickly take you and move you out of this illusion. That is His promise to you.

With this Incarnation, you can come Home. You need to go deep within, and you stay situated deep within and just move. Sometimes you have to cry, and sometimes you have to scream. But He is going to take you very swiftly and very fast into union with Him. He is going to take you, but you have to go deep and stay focused. Try to hear. Stay with Him deep within. Become serious. *Stay with Him deep within.*

You have to learn to get to that point where you stay deep within, because you cannot get where you need to go

Notes:
_____

_____

_____

spiritually when you go in and out, and in and out, and in and out of depth. The only reason you come out of your depth is because you are afraid to give up your own separate way, and if you stay within, you know you are going to do it with God. You will just keep going and going if you stay within with God, and your illusions fall away as you are changing, changing, changing. Your illusory being doesn't like to do that; you are afraid to change so much, because then you cannot grab on to the illusion again.

But God has come and He is saying to do it this way! He has come to take you very, very fast. When will you hear? He is saying it very, very clearly, and I am just simply repeating it for Him once again. This is what you must do.

You go through seminars and workshops, and your fist is closed tightly, and He is prying your fingers free from the illusion. Your fingers are pried free from the illusion to get you to the point where you will finally just surrender and let go and give up.

Just come within to where the Lord in your heart resides! Be deep in prayer. Don't leave that place. Stay there. Let God be the only answer, the only focus.

You will still be able to live your life. Your life will actually get better and better the closer you are to God. It will become simpler, it will become richer and much more rewarding than you could ever possibly make your own life be on

Notes:

your own. It will be different than how you would have done it, but everything will be the way you really wanted it to be.

The goal of all of the spiritual work that you do on the Path to Ultimate Freedom, the goal of Lord Gourasana's teachings, is to come to this point of staying deep inside with Him. *The goal is to gather all of your focus and all of your attention and turn it within to where the Lord is.* Turn it to where the connection to that power within is, to where that special assistance from God is, to where you can feel that connection deep within. Turn your focus and attention there. For those of you that are ready to call upon Lord Gourasana, this is a very powerful thing. You can call on God however you want, but the Incarnation is here, and calling on the name Gourasana will speed everything up for you. You will feel the Father when you call the name Gourasana. Call, "Lord." Learn to live in that depth. Don't come out, because if you come out, you are coming out to take a breath of the illusion.

Coming to this place of living in the depth with Him is what you are all working toward. Once you come to this place, then my job is done with you, because then He has you directly. Then you are in the Gateway; you are on your way Home. You are beginning to then be filled by the presence of the Lord, and He has you. You will not be able to give up, because He will then be taking you. And that is my ecstasy.

Notes:
_____

_____

_____

183

The movement, once you are focused within, is swift. There is not a whole lot of understanding that you need to have at this point in your transformation; it is faster than your mind can comprehend. There are not a whole lot of issues; there is just movement.

When you come up against something, you go within. You find out what it is. You find out the answer of what to do about it. You do it, and then you move on. You have already said, "Yes, I give my existence. I give everything." Now you go through the process of just moving: one illusion after the other just flying away. Go deep. Stay deep. Stay focused. Gather all of your attention and turn it toward the Lord.

Read *Breaking the Cycle of Birth and Death*. Read it again and again. It tells you practically everything that you need to know. Those words are alive. They are true. They direct you. He is speaking to you. He is telling you.

Don't waste any more time. Go within. Go deep. Stay focused. Be with Him. Don't be frivolous. You can't be frivolous when you are deep within. And if you can only go deep for one hour a day, then go deep for one hour. Then the next week, make it an hour and a half. And then the next month, make it two hours. Set a goal for yourself and start to practice the presence of the Lord. The Lord is deep within and that is where he resides: deep within your heart.

Notes:
_____

_____

_____

Concepts

Spoken on August 28, 2006

As soon as words of guidance come out of my mouth, people form concepts about them. As much as the words in this talk are clearing up concepts, they are also creating concepts. I want you to be careful about creating concepts. I want you to just be with these words of guidance and let yourself live with them for a while and come into realization from your own experience using this guidance. Try to really understand it deeply, by experience.

One example of a concept that came out of what I said in this *Break-Free Message* series is something I heard one disciple say. The disciple said, "I can't wait to tell my friends that they don't have to do any more workshops, that they don't have to work on themselves. All they have to do is let go." But that is the farthest thing from the truth. You have to do so much work on yourself. It is by doing that work that the things that you need to let go of, come to the surface. If you do not work on yourself, then how is it that you even know what you have to let go of? You have to continue to work on yourself so that everything that you need to let go of comes to the surface. And then one by one by

Notes:

one, everything comes to the surface, and you let go of it. But you have got to drive everything from the core of your being to the surface so that you can let go of all of the illusions.

Another concept I heard was from a disciple speaking to another disciple. The first disciple said, "I've got to get to the bottom of this illusion." And the other disciple said, "No, you don't. You just have to let go." Well, first you have to find out what it is you are trying to let go of. And that person was needing to find out what they needed to let go of. Then, they could let go of it. Or, perhaps that person had a big wall in front of them, and what they needed to do was let go in meditation and push through that wall, and that was how they were going to get to the bottom of it. So a better thing to have said was, "You are going to have to meditate and push through that wall, because it's been sitting there for so long, and you've been stuck in it for so long."

You need to be in touch with the person that you are speaking to. You can't just whimsically say something to someone. You can't whimsically say, "Well, just let go." You have to know the person that you are speaking to and what it is that they are going through. You can't just say something to someone out of nowhere. You have to know what is going on with that person if you are going to give some advice, suggestions, or guidance. You can't just say, "Everybody just let go." If someone needs to get to the bottom of

Notes:

_____

_____

_____

something, maybe they are trying to find out with their awareness if they are even at a point where what they have to do is let go. Once they realize, "Oh, I just have to let go," then they will just let go. Or, maybe they're up against a big wall and they need to realize that they need to meditate and push through that.

Myself, I'm moving at a very, very rapid speed into more and more consciousness. I'm not moving through illusion. I'm moving into higher and higher consciousness, and I do that through awareness. Even prior to this time, when there was illusion within this being that needed to be moved through, first I had to understand; then it came to the point that it was just done through awareness. And sometimes there would come a point where there was just something in the way. The flow, the rapid speed of movement that I was in, just stopped for a moment. When for several days, the rapid speed of movement came to a stopping point, I would be searching, "What is wrong, what is wrong? The movement has stopped." Then I would remember at some point, "Oh, the movement has stopped. That must mean I have to let go." And I would realize, "Oh, I have to let go. Okay. There is nothing I can do. I just have to let go." And once I realized I had to let go, then I would be moving again. And at some point, a realization would come in of what had to be let go of or moved out of the way.

Notes:

_____

_____

This letting go is going to come into realization inside of you all in many, many ways. Once you understand it clearly, then, when you are helping someone, you will understand how to use the words, "just let go," and they will mean something to the person that you are speaking to. Because you have realized this teaching, you will really understand what you are talking about when you are speaking those words to another person. You will understand the predicament that another person is in, and you will understand if it is proper to say, "Just let go. You just have to let go." And the person will be able to hear you; it will be the appropriate thing to say, rather than just casually passing by someone when they say to you, "I have to get to the bottom of something," and saying "Just let go. You don't have to get to the bottom of anything."

I don't want you to take my teachings and my guidance and whimsically say things to people like "Oh, you don't have to work on anything anymore. You can just let go." That is not what I am talking about.

In this series, I made a talk about pushing down the walls that come up. It is about when you are just moving and moving with God, and then a wall comes up and your darkness is there again, and you have to push it down. You push, push, and push until the light comes again. After I made that talk, someone said to me, "Well, I guess there is

Notes:

_____

_____

nothing to do anymore except just move, and then if I get knocked in the head and something comes up, then I'll just move through it."

That is not exactly what I said either. What I said and what Gourasana said is, "Do not become complacent at any point, until you are carried away by the presence of the Lord." So what this person is telling me is that they are just going to go about their life and just do their service and carry on, and if something bonks them on the head or if they hit into their darkness or into an illusion, then they will do some work. *That is being complacent.* Where is the prayer, "Please, I want to go faster. Lord, I know I am not all of the way Home"? Where is falling asleep in prayer? Where are all the rest of my teachings that I have been speaking? This person has misunderstood my teaching about pushing down walls to mean to not do anything unless you get conked on the head and all of a sudden there is a wall, and then you do the work.

I just want to warn you that what the mind wants to do with the truth, or with anything that I say, is form a concept. I want you all to be spiritual grownups and be deeper than that. Be a little more serious. For example, for someone that is unworthy, it is true that they have to let go of it, but they also have a lot of meditation work and breaking down walls, and they have a lot of action to take to break their

Notes:
_____

_____

189

habits: They have a lot to go through to let go. They have to be letting go constantly. They have meditation work to do; that is a very hard wall to break down. In that case, the letting go is to keep consistently working on whatever it is every day that you need to work on in order to break that illusion of unworthiness, and then at a certain point, you will be able to see it because there will be so much light. You will be able to see it so clearly that you will just say, "I'm done with that."

But the letting go will be a result of a lot of pushing through wall after wall after wall and confrontation of that illusion. You have to let go to do that work; you have to face that work head on. And you have let go every time you do that work. For one who has a lot of unworthiness, it takes a very courageous person to really find their way to the other side. You let go, and then you let go some more, and then you let go some more, and you let go some more, and you let go some more, and finally you let go of it all. You can't just say to that person, whimsically, "You can just let go." But of course, there are a lot of things that you can just let go of.

Be Done
with the Illusion

Spoken on June 26, 2007

What the path was all about in the beginning of the Mission – and is about now – is to give up your separate will, to give up your control, to give up your ego, and to give up your mind chatter. It is not about issues and feelings or about how people think the path should be. It is not about hanging on to control.

Once you get to the point where you have released all of your excess anger and excess unworthiness, then what there is to do is just put your hands out and say, "Father, Father, please take me, I give myself to You completely, entirely, utterly. I give You my whole heart and soul, my body, my mind, my control, my separate will." You do not hang on to anything. You just are saying, "Father, take me, now, please." And as you are saying it, you are stretching your hands toward Him so He can take your hand and take you.

You have to give up your control. You have to give up your separate will. You have to give up your mind and all of its traps. You don't *work through* all of that. You don't

Notes:
_____

_____

_____

stay on the floor in meditation and keep thinking whether you are going to surrender or work through all of your control. You are on the floor praying to God sincerely, from your heart, to take you. The secret is that you have to pray, "Father, take me," and at the same time that you say that, you are offering yourself completely to Him: no hanging on.

There is work that you need to do on the floor with opening up your being to allow the energy of the Lord to move through you, wave after wave after wave. When you do that kind of meditation with His presence and energy moving through you, He is just moving you through so much illusion that you don't even know what is happening. All you know is you just got closer to God. *That is not going down an avenue of issues.* The prayer is, "Father, take me. Father, take me. Please take away my control. Please take away all of my mind traps. Please take away my ego. Please take away my free will."

You are allowing Him, His transformational energy, to just move through you intensely, wave after wave after wave after wave. You may feel like you are in control of it, but you have to get to the point where He becomes in control of that energy and you are no longer in control of it and you are letting go to ... "Uh oh ... something's happening." *You have to let Him take over:* "Father, please take me; I only want You, and I give everything, my whole self, to You. I am

Notes:

_____

_____

_____

here for You. I am not here to sit here and work on my feelings and all of this stuff, I am here to be taken by You, and I am here to go Home at the soonest possible moment."

You will understand this the more you practice it. You will go really fast the more you practice this. The more you practice this, the faster you are going to go and the faster Gourasana is going to be able to take you. It doesn't have to take fifteen years – it can take just four or five.

You have to let go of everything in order to go into God's Kingdom. Everything. If you trust God and let go of everything – even let go of your pains, your mental issues, your judgments, and your physical pains – He will take you. You just have to let it all go and reach out to the Father and say, "Father, please, I am ready now; please take me." At that moment when you are one hundred percent "Just take me," He takes you. And so many of your problems are just lifted by God in the moment that you ask for it and you mean it. Right in that moment, when you really, really mean it, then you can come Home. But not if you are hanging on to anything of the illusion.

Let me put it this way; your prayer should be:

Lord, take away my control, please, take it. Smash it. I have no need for it. If I hang on to it, that means I won't be with You. I have no need for it, because I only want You. And if I hang on to control, having it be the way I want it to be, even a little bit the way I want it to be, then that little bit will separate me from You. So, please, rip it away. Rip away my control, please; take it. And Lord, please, please take my separate will. I give it to You. Please take it; I give it to You. No more separate will, because the separate will that I hang on to separates me from being with You, and I only want to be with You. Please, Lord, rip away my separate will, despite myself. Please take away my separate will. Please take me despite my faults. Take me despite anything that I might say out of my mouth contrary, because my truest desire is I want to be with You fully and completely at the soonest possible moment. I want You, my Father. Please, where I am blind, let me see. And let me please see in a way that I am awe-struck and so I can immed-iately let go. Because, Father, I want to be with You. I don't want to control anything anymore. It is useless to hang on to my control. It is useless to hang on to my separate free will. I want to give back my free will. I want to let go of all of my control right now. Please, just rip it away.

This is the way you have to approach the Father. And you have to let go of those things as you pray those things. You see, you are hanging on. You are trying to go to God, and nothing is wrong with your spiritual development except that you are hanging on. You are also hanging on

Notes:

194

desperately to your suffering. You would rather have your suffering than just "Father, take me, I give it all to You. I am coming into your arms right now and I am never ever, ever, ever, ever, ever leaving."

This is where you have to come to in your spiritual transformation. And it doesn't have to take a whole lot of time. *It is a decision.* I pray your fear doesn't stop you and that you come at the soonest possible moment into the arms of the Lord, free of all of the illusory things that have you bound. It is a choice that you have to make. When you make that choice, you will be set free and He will take you.

So what is it going to be? When? Or do you just want to take care of all of your hurt feelings and become a better being of illusion? What is that all about? God wants to take you out of this place, because it is endless, endless suffering and hurt feelings. You are not going to get very far by just healing your feelings; you want to get out of this place of illusion. So you have to let go and give up and surrender.

Good luck, and I am praying for you all to take the fast road and just come. Give your self to God. It doesn't matter what you feel, it doesn't matter how much it hurts. You tell Him that you are willing to do anything, so then let it hurt. Let your feelings hurt, but go to God and let it all go. Be done with it. *Be done with it.*

Notes:

_____

_____

_____

LIVE YOUR LIFE AS GOD
WOULD HAVE IT

Cindy: Gourasana, can you tell us about complete and total surrender in our lives – what that means?
Gourasana: Yes. First you must give up everything as you would have it in your lifetime – all your plans, all your conceptions, for the future. How you want it to be; how you think it should be. You must give all of this up – even as you conceive spiritual life to be. Some have certain conceptions of how spiritual life will be, and they must give up these conceptions. Whatever the conceptions, they all must go. You have so many conceptions. A turning point comes in your spiritual life where you have so completely given up your plans that you are prepared to die; you will gladly give up your life for awareness. Attaining awareness has become that critical, that you will not only give up your plans and hopes for the future, but you will give up your future in this existence. To come to that point is essential.

And then the next step, the harder step, is to continue to live, but live as you need to live to become aware, without considering – is it pleasurable or not pleasurable, is there fear or not, is there suffering or not, is it increasing my distress or not? You just do what another will has you to do. You give up your will, and you do what the Universe would have you do.

That is all. If you can take these two steps, then you will succeed. That is serious. That is complete surrender: to give up your will, to surrender to a higher will.

Live Your Life as a 59'er

Spoken by The Lady on April 13, 2008
at The Intensive

*If someone truly wishes to leave this plane of illusion
in this lifetime, then you do not need to be his guardian,
because he will see to it that he leaves.*

GOURASANA, *Breaking The Cycle of Birth and Death,*
Quote #59

Kalindi wants everyone who is on the path Home to God to walk the path as a strong and sturdy "59'er": someone who captures the essence of Quote #59. Being a 59'er means you follow the guidance of Kalindi with determination and precision. Her guidance tells you how to defeat the illusion and surrender to God. And as you do this, the presence and love of God will pour through you into this love-starved world. So every day, follow the guidance of Kalindi to become freer from the illusion and closer to the love of God.

That's all I did, and that is all the Core* did. I followed the footsteps and guidance of Kalindi, I listened to

---

* The Core is the group of seven people who founded this Mission with Gourasana.

Notes:

_____

_____

_____

and followed what Gourasana said, and I never said "no." It wasn't easy. Many times I wanted to say "no" and leave the work. But I couldn't leave, because I trusted and I had faith from knowing it was God that was happening. In addition, by following the guidance of Kalindi I was becoming freer of the illusion, directly experiencing the truth within, and realizing the reality of God.

So I am encouraging you to walk the path as I did and to find it in your heart to trust, to willingly surrender your free will to the Lord, and to always say "Yes!" to the guidance of Kalindi. You must turn your back on the ways of the illusion with decisiveness and desire for the truth. You must willingly endure the difficulties of transformation and maintain a positive attitude. It is true that there is a price to pay, but the rewards are priceless. And you can always be encouraged, because one thing is for sure – with God it always gets better.

Most importantly, you must never give up. Do not even consider giving up. You must pass through the dark nights of the soul, and you must maturely accept the fact that there will be more than one dark night of the soul to cross through. Remain on your knees, knowing that you are a fool, you are lost, you are bound by the illusion and, in the bigger picture, you truly don't know what is really going on. You just know you want Home, and to make it Home you

Notes:

_____

_____

know you need the guidance from someone who is empowered to see the illusion. Kalindi clearly *sees* the illusion; Kalindi *knows* the illusion. And her guidance can help you break free and come Home to God.

> *How will you break free from the illusion?*
> *It is not possible without assistance.*
> GOURASANA

Some people misunderstand what it means to be a 59'er. They have mistakenly concluded that being a 59'er means that they can decide when in their transformation they no longer need guidance from their spiritual master, or they think they actually know better than their master what they need to do. Be careful. This is a dangerous misunderstanding, because you are in illusion, and from your state of illusion you are not the one to determine what is best for your spiritual advancement. Become and remain humble. It is a fact that your spiritual master will always be ahead of you. To become free of illusion, you need to not only surrender to God, but also you need to surrender to the guidance of the spiritual master who is taking you to God. Obedience to the guidance of the master destroys the "I know better" ego that is actually separating you from God.

I didn't say "no" to my spiritual master. Kalindi held the light and I followed. I am never, ever, without my spiritual master. It comes down to simple trust and faith. As far

Notes:

as I am concerned, sincere devotion and obedience to the master is the same as sincere devotion and obedience to God. Surrender to the guidance of Kalindi led me to surrender to God. Now I live a devoted life as a strong and sturdy 59'er who follows the guidance of Kalindi. I am continuously surrendering and becoming freer and closer to God every day: *Everything* has been given to me; *Nothing* is ever missing.

I suggest you read this book as direct guidance from Kalindi – because it is just that. As you reap the benefits of living the life of a strong and sturdy 59'er, there will be profound joy, gratitude, and love in your heart. Because you will have directly experienced the value of following vital guidance and your soul will have recognized the presence of a living master who speaks the truth straight and can take you Home – her name is Kalindi.

Follow her guidance, do your work, and receive the blessings of God.

Notes:

Determination Non-Stop

Spoken on September 28, 2007

You need to live your path with constant determination. There is so much to be had here in Miracle of Love, so much of God, so much with each other, that people are satisfied with the connections that they do have. They are so full. But then people are not being driven to their knees, working constantly on breaking themselves free: "I have to have Him. That is all I want, is Him! I don't want to just be freer and freer and closer and closer. I want Him so badly. I am so determined now! I am just so determined. I am making my bedroom into a sanctuary of meditation and prayer. And every time I get in there, I am just going to meditate and beg the Lord, "*Please,* I just want to be with You. Please help me!"

People have to be constantly working to break themselves free. But people not only need to be working on breaking themselves free, but they also need to be coming closer to the Lord. People need to be striving to come closer to the Lord so they can feel the Lord, and that at the end of

Notes:

every day they can feel the Lord more. And if they can't feel the Lord more, then when they get in bed, they are begging, "Oh my God, where are You? I need to feel You more! Where are You?" They are going to sleep like that, so that by the time they wake up, the first thing in their consciousness is, "Where are You? Where are You?" Then they are meditating as soon as they get up to see if they can find the Lord. First they find their connection with the Lord in the morning, and then they write their RE's*. But they cannot start the day without that connection to the Lord.

You do not have this type of constant determination going on. You can't start and stop and start and stop if you want to find the Lord. Determination has to start and stay, non-stop determination for the presence of the Lord to fill you! Don't be satisfied until you are filled all the way with His presence. *All the way.* All the way and then more, and then more, and then more. Being filled with the energy of the Lord is a very personal thing between the seeker and God. Without non-stop determination, this will not happen all the way.

The number one teaching is to be begging for the Lord, with determination. It takes some time to get to that point. But the seeker should be striving to get to the point of

---

* Kalindi's guidance is to meditate in the morning and take time to write down, in order to keep a calm and empty mind, things that come to you that you need to remember, which she terms "RE's."

Notes: _____

_____

_____

having so much desire for the Lord: so much desire to have the Lord, to feel the Lord, to become consumed by the Lord, to be filled by the presence of the Lord. And get to the point that it is not okay with you unless that occurs.

In addition, you should get to the point that it is not okay with you that others don't have the opportunity to have God. You should get to the point where all that your life is about is your livelihood, the care of your body, the care for your children (if you have them), and that others have the opportunity to also have God. Your life is about you doing everything that your heart can do to find the Lord and draw Him to you. You are begging, letting go, surrendering, doing whatever you have to do with the greatest non-stop determination, because all you want is to be with the Lord once again – Home. This kind of determination must be found!

Notes:

Be Connected to God

Spoken on September 14, 2007

When you are going about your transformation, day after day, week after week, month after month, year after year, the idea is to meditate when you need to meditate. Everybody pretty much works at a job during the day, so you need to meditate in the morning or at night. When you meditate, you need to meditate until that session is over and you are in a calm state and you are connected to the presence of the Lord. Then you get up and go about your work throughout the day, or you go to sleep in a calm state.

The idea is not that you work on yourself all day long spiritually and drive yourself crazy the whole day while you are at work. When you go to work, you go to work and you are connected to the presence of the Lord and situated in your awareness, at whatever level that might be. You go through your day in a conscious state connected to God.

Don't go through the day being driven crazy by all of your illusions. You may be feeling the intensity from God, but that is different than feeling all of your issues and problems all day long. That is not how to do the work.

Notes:
_____

_____

_____

There was a point in David Swanson's transformation when he had to meditate once in the morning and once at night in order to get through the day. Because the intensity of God pushing on him was so intense, he had to release his emotions twice a day. But when he was working, he was conscious, he was sweet, and he was loving and giving. He was engaged in whatever work he was doing throughout the day. He was very giving and very present, and he was connecting with each person that he encountered during the day. When it was time for meditation, it was time for meditation; and it was a serious meditation. It is not that you do not feel anything of your transformation during the day, but your focus is not there. Your focus is on paying attention to your job and being in your God-connected, aware state.

You have to see for yourself when you need to meditate. You may need to meditate sometimes more and sometimes less, depending on what is going on with you. It is a very individual thing. Sometimes you may have to meditate for five hours in a day, and then sometimes you have to meditate just for the one hour that I have guided you to do in the evening, plus your weekly three-hour meditations with your community or at your Center. You really need to pay attention to when you need to medi-

Notes:

tate. And when you are walking around in your daily life, you need to be in your connected state of consciousness and in the love of God. This is important for you to understand.

Notes:

Ever-Increasing Love and Ecstasy

Spoken on March 30, 2007

Returning Home to the Source is ever-increasing love and ecstasy. That happens while you are alive. To be filled with the presence of the Lord is everything. Your true being resides within the presence of the Lord. When you are consumed by the presence of the Lord, the illusion has to move away from you. The more you let go of the illusions that have you bound, the more you work on the being of illusion to see it and to let go of it, the more the presence of the Lord can fill you and surround you. *But you have to let go.* It is an endeavor that needs to be a constant prayer, a constant asking, and constant searching.

For those of you that are so fortunate as to feel the presence of the Lord, don't be satisfied with a little bit of the presence of the Lord. Don't rest until you are carried away by the presence of the Lord, consumed by the presence of the Lord.

Truly becoming immersed in the presence of the Lord is not an easy endeavor, but it is possible. So many of you are

Notes:

_____

_____

_____

so filled with the presence of the Lord already, and in that presence you feel your true being. But the endeavor must continue. The endeavor to break free from all illusion must continue in order to be filled by the presence of the Lord. That is when you will feel your Home. It is ever increasing; it just goes on and on and on. The love just increases more and more and more. It is love and ecstasy beyond your comprehension.

It is important that you don't let up on the endeavor to break free. Your prayer has to become moment-by-moment prayer. Be in moment-by-moment prayer until you are in a constant state of prayer: "Lord, please take me. Lord, please, I want only to be with you, Lord, please." In order for you to have success in breaking the cycle of birth and death and returning Home, this has to become one hundred percent of your desire. You have to get to the point where you have burning desire at one hundred percent in order to make it. And you don't stop that burning desire.

You may have certain times where you let go, or certain shifts in your consciousness where you did have one hundred percent burning endeavor, and you broke through into more light. You have to have a lot of endeavor and a lot of desire just to break through into more light – what to speak of returning into the presence of the Lord. I am not just talking about God walking next to you like some people

Notes:

talk about; I am talking about being filled with the presence of the Lord. That endeavor must not stop.

There are people that have been traveling this path for quite some time, and you need to really let go now. You need to go deeper than you have ever gone. You need to start to call upon the presence of the Lord. And those of you that have not been here on the path as long, do the same. Go deeper. Go deeper in earnest and pray to be filled by the presence of the Lord.

Do your meditation work. When you meditate, go for it! Don't just be idle. Go for it whether that means that you sit in silence and your awareness moves, or you are on the floor screaming and crying. Have one hundred percent desire at every single meditation.

When you do the Modern-Day Meditation and you find out information about what you need to do to get out of an illusion, you need to listen to that information, because you need to find your way out of the illusion. You know the things that have you bound. You have to have great courage to let these things go or to change your situation.

When you come to an Intensive, you build up so much desire, and at a point you are just at one hundred per-cent desire. Then you break through into a connection. Now I am talking about getting an eternal connection that won't break. That means having a lot of small connections one

Notes:

_____

_____

after the next after the next after the next. It means being in constant movement. Don't be satisfied with just a little bit of the presence of God. For sure don't be satisfied if you are not feeling the presence of the Lord, because you are missing out on everything. To miss out on that love and that fulfillment of your heart's desire when it's so possible to have Him is pretty crazy.

Don't sit around for days not feeling Him and not feeling His presence increasing, increasing, increasing. Ask for more, more, more: "Lord, more. Please. I want only You. Please, more." Meditate like that.

When you are at home, do one hour of meditation daily. That is a lot of serious prayer. A lot of connection can happen in that one hour if you are deep. During that hour, you should go deep and find your connection to Him and let it flow more. And if you can't find your connection, then cry and pray and do what you need to do to open up more.

You need to meditate every day for some part of the day. Before going to bed is a good time to pray for the presence of the Lord. Don't go to sleep until you can feel it. And once you feel it, then go to sleep in the peace of His perfection and His timing. But I wouldn't go to sleep if I weren't feeling the Lord. And I wouldn't hang around just watching television and taking a break – if you want to break free. Constantly hanging out and taking a break and watching

Notes:
_____

_____

TV with your extra time is not a good thing to do. It's okay to watch TV for a break once in a while, but if that is what you do at night when you're not at meditation, then that is not a good thing. If you have time and you are sitting around, you should meditate. You have got to get this kind of burning desire inside of yourself. Remember, the illusion wants to stop you. The illusion wants to stop you constantly. It is constantly after you. You have to be one step ahead of the illusion.

"Constant Change" is God's nickname, constant change, constant movement forward. Constant movement forward! Maybe change causes you to become afraid constantly, but go forward anyway. Maybe in meditation you hit upon places within, where you are just afraid to go any deeper. But scream, and go deeper anyway.

What there is to do is to become filled with desire. Be consumed by desire to be filled by the presence of the Lord, and do not stop until that has happened. Once you are filled with the presence of the Lord, your connection just keeps becoming brighter and brighter with more and more love. I am telling you it is possible. It is possible because of Gourasana, His power and His presence.

When you feel Gourasana, you feel the Father, the energy of the part of God that is the Father. That is a special benediction that Gourasana has brought in. You can

Notes:

just climb into His arms and just be held. He doesn't have to be in a physical body for you to climb into His arms.

So when will you start to climb into His arms so He can hold you so tight that you never ever, ever, ever can even get away for one second? That is what your true desire is. Crawl into the arms of God. Crawl into the arms of the Lord. Let Him give you everything that you are. And you let go of everything that you are not. It's a two-sided situation. Desire is everything.

Notes:

Fully Aware, Fully Awake, and Fully Connected

Spoken on October 28, 2007

Instead of saying, "I have so much awareness," and instead of thinking, "I have so much awareness; look at how much awareness I have," you should look at how far along you need to come. Instead of trying to prove you have awareness and have people know how much awareness you have, look at how far along you need to come.

One way that you can defeat the part of the being of illusion that wants recognition is to take a position of humility and look at the distance you have yet to go: "I have a lot to learn, and all of these people that I am with have a lot to teach me. I know that. I can feel inside of myself that I have a lot to learn."

In this way you can follow in The Lady's footsteps. When she was around Kalindi, and David Swanson*, and around Gourasana, she would soak up everything like a

---

* David Swanson was the man who gave his life for Gourasana to manifest in this world.

Notes:

sponge. She knew that she didn't know. Still today, when she is around Kalindi, she is still like a sponge; she knows that anything that comes out of my mouth, she needs to hear. It is like that with the entire Core. You can use the same approach as the Core did.

It is the being of illusion that wants recognition that is thinking, "I have so much awareness." It is not the true being that thinks that.

On the other hand, there are times when the true being needs to get strong and it needs to recognize, "Yes, I do have awareness. I do know." Because the three most obvious signs of the illusion* are screaming so much and so loudly, causing the true self to have so much doubt. So it goes both ways. Sometimes you have to do one thing, and sometimes you have to do another thing. There are so many concepts, and there are so many different ways that you need to go.

You need to wake up. You need to forget about the issues. I can't say that enough. The issues are not even a part, practically speaking, of the spiritual work that I'm trying to teach you. Issues are so minute and practically have nothing to do at all with transformation. You have to worry about the illusion that is after you and how you are going to deal with it. Issues are just bothersome little things on the sidelines.

---

* The three most obvious signs are judgments, negative thoughts, and discouragement.

Notes:

_____

_____

_____

You have to worry about being wide awake all the time so you can see what is going on around you. You need to pay attention to what is affecting your spiritual being and your ability to stay awake and aware. You have to have the ability to see what is pulling you away from God, and you have to have the ability to be with God at that moment.

You all have the ability to be with God all the time, but you just fall asleep. You get sleepy and you go away from God. You move away from God all throughout the day. Your awareness isn't strong enough. Your consciousness isn't strong enough to stay awake.

You have to practice staying awake. Stay awake! Stay focused and stay awake at every moment. Practice that. Wear a watch that you set to beep every hour to remind you to stay awake. The Lady used an egg timer. Gourasana told her to get one and just keep turning it every hour and to pay attention. She did it. She was a teacher and she used an egg timer; she turned it every hour and made sure that she was awake to her spiritual awareness. Awake and aware, and connected to God: "No illusion around me. With God. No illusion trying to get me. Okay, on with the next hour."

You have to practice staying awake. If you are not awake and aware, the illusion is going to capture you in so many ways, in the matter of 15 minutes. Because you are sleepy and not focused on God, you are, of course, going to

Notes:

216

be captured by the issues and then you are going to be in the realm of issues. Then you have completely forgotten about God. You are not even in your awake spiritual consciousness. You are just trapped in this world of the mundane where every little thing bothers you. That is the material world, the material world of mundane issues. If you were awake and aware and connected to God, and feeling that, you would be in a way higher consciousness. You would be in a way higher consciousness where you would just deal with the issues for what they are and do the necessary to carry on. You would not let yourself go away from God. You would be dealing with the things of this world from a way higher place.

I suggest that everybody that is hearing this talk, right now, *immediately*, live that way right now. Change the way that you live and come into a higher, more awake consciousness, immediately. Now! Be in a higher consciousness, connected to God. Practice that. This isn't just an exercise. This is a lifelong practice, until you become fully aware, and fully awake, and fully with God. That is what you are striving for, and now this is what I am telling you to do to get there.

If you have to take a cold shower every morning when you wake up, there is nothing wrong with that. I did that for seven or eight years – woke up at four in the

Notes:
_____

_____

_____

morning and took a cold shower to wake up out of the sleepiness that sleep causes. I would wake up every morning calling God's name. Then I went into the cold shower. You can have a cool shower. Just make sure there is no warm water in it at all; not tepid water, but use water that is on the cool side. Put your head under the water and just scream, "Gourasana, Gourasana, Gourasana, I'm awake, I'm awake, I'm awake, please keep me awake all day! I want to be awake, awake, awake!"

Start your day awake. Do not wake up with whatever issues are on your mind and how you don't feel that good, and you are depressed, and with five or ten issues on your mind. No. No, no, no! Wake up with the glory of God on your mind. "Yes, thank you that I'm awake, that I didn't die during my sleep, because I need to stay alive, because I need to move forward. I'm not done yet. Thank you that I'm awake. Another day, I'm awake. And now when I get out of the shower, then I'm going to be aware. Thank you that I can be aware. And now I'm going to sit in a chair, and I'm going to meditate for fifteen minutes to deepen my connection. And I have my writing tablet next to me in case there are things on my mind from when I was asleep at night and I can write them down – a little reminder, so I don't forget. Then back to my meditation, until I don't have anything that I need to remember and I can just sit with God for five

Notes:

minutes and connect. And then start my day happy that I'm connected with God. And whatever I have to face that day, I'm going to face from a connected place."

Don't let the three most obvious signs beat you down! Start your day connected, not beaten down. I hope you can understand this. You should read this talk over and over and over again. This is the new morning, afternoon, evening, whenever-you-need-to-listen-to-it talk. And if you do what I am saying, your life will be different.

At the beginning of the talk, I told you how you can get the part of the being of illusion that wants recognition out of the way, just by being humble and knowing that you don't know anything at all. Be humble. And now wake up!

Do you see? My guidance comes out on all of my talks. Hearing and doing this humility practice is what it means to listen to my guidance. Now, who will do this? It may not be accurate for everyone to do this. But for those that it is accurate for, try it.

It is accurate for everyone to stay awake, stay aware, and stay connected! So if you have a different way to do that, do it. But you need to stay awake, aware, connected. You need to be like that, and you need to live in a higher consciousness. Stop getting stuck in the plane of illusion with the issues. Just stop it. That is just stuff in the material world that needs to be dealt with. That is all that it is. What

Notes: _____

_____

you are striving for is to have higher consciousness, be awake, aware, and connected all of the time. And then every day go deeper, and then deeper. If you can't get any deeper, just meditate and go deeper and deeper. And then you hit against a wall of illusion, and of course you are crying, because you cannot feel the Lord as deeply as you want. Or there is a block and you have to move that block to go further, deeper within to the Lord.

I love you. It is all possible!

But you can't have a lazy streak in your body. You just can't. If you do, you have to start working on that. What I'm telling you to do in this talk is going to take care of that lazy part too.

Come on, let's go. You want God? Okay, come on! Let's be with God. You have to do your part with this practice and with letting go of everything you have to let go of that's binding you. It's not a mystery. And I'm guiding you what to do.

At some point you are not going to have to use a cold shower. It is just going to be automatic. You are just awake all the time. My consciousness never, ever goes to sleep. It is fully aware, fully awake, all the time. So, come and join me! Join me in the land of God.

I know that you know that it is everything because you are already starting to taste it. Just come on, all the way.

Notes:

If you want to know about *real* enlightenment – the *real* thing – this is going to lead you to it. This is going to lead you there. So stop looking out into the sky, or wherever you are looking, for anything. And *wake up*. Wake up! Then you will be on your way to awakening in the real sense of what it *really* is.

You will find out many things through your many, many awakenings until you are fully awake and fully aware in the love of God. Many, many experiences of enlightenment are going to happen to you. On your way to enlightenment you will have all different experiences, but you have got to start here. You have to be fully awake. You have to become fully awake and fully aware and fully connected. And then you will be walking on the path toward where you are going – Home.

I'm trying to get you to walk straight. *Follow me.* I can take you where it is you want to go.

You are going to have to also do your own part fully. You are going to have to find your own way within the path that I'm guiding you on. It's not that I can tell you every single detail of what you have to do and what you have to let go of every second of every day. You are going to have to find your way within the guidance that I am giving you.

I can show you the way. I am shining bright lights everywhere. "Over here. Over here. Over here." I'm speaking so many ways of how to go through so many things. Grab hold to my words and my guidance. Just keep grabbing for some part that you can hear, that you can listen to, and makes sense to you, and that you can do.

I have to still tell you that you have to be awake and aware and connected. You just can't *not* do that; you have to do that in order to even walk on the path. You have to get on the path and walk straight.

You will fall off a few times, but there is so much help that you won't be off the straight path very long before you hear another talk from Kalindi, or someone tells you to listen to this talk. Just lock yourself in your bedroom and listen to this talk over and over and over again until you wake up again. Because at some point you are just going to go and put yourself in the shower. And then you are going to wake up and everything is going to be okay again. You will be with God again. You will remember because you will wake up. You will say, "Aha, I'm awake again. I am back with God and I am back with my awareness, and I'm back awake. Thank God. I don't want to fall off the road again."

When you fall off the road, you don't even know how you fell off the road. The illusion just got you. Or you just looked at a flower and said, "Oh, I have to go smell that flower," and you thought you were just going to go for a second to smell the flower and all of a sudden it's two weeks

Notes:

later and you are completely into the world of issues and whatever goes on out there. You tripped over your shoelaces, and you are completely swallowed up by the illusion in every way in which the illusion gets you. You got covered over, and you forgot that there was even a path to God that you were walking down.

The *last thing you want to do* is even get off on some road: "I'm not taking any cold showers anymore. I don't want to do that. And, I just want to sleep anyway. I don't want to be awake. I am tired of being awake. I'm tired of being aware. I'm tired of it all. I don't want to do it, and everybody leave me alone." A month goes by and everybody is leaving you alone because you said, "Leave me alone." Everybody is leaving you alone, including God, because that is your free will, and you told God, "Leave me alone." So everybody is leaving you alone while you are in the illusion, lost, afraid, angry, and hateful, thinking everybody else is wrong and you are right. And everybody else has all this love, and all this care, and all this concern, and you are looking at everyone thinking, "You guys are crazy. You all look the same, and you're like hawks that are coming after me. I don't want anybody coming after me, and I don't want to hear anything about God." So you bury yourself deeper and deeper and deeper until you can't even feel any love, and you can't even feel anything about God. And God

Notes:

_____

_____

_____

is just backing off like He always does, because He has given you free will. So there you are, sitting in your free will, quite alone, quite stubborn, quite in the personality of your ego, suffering like crazy, and not even admitting that you are suffering. You are sitting there, hard as a brick, pretending to be nice all the way back in your illusory self.

You did that to yourself. The Lady used to do this. You wouldn't believe it. I just refer you to The Lady so you can have some faith. "If The Lady did this, I am sure there is going to be some hope for me."

You need to try to listen to the help. Listen to the people that are trying to talk to you. When you get like that, that is the struggle: to listen to people who are trying to help you. It is part of the path; you fall off the path. That is why if someone tells you, "Listen to this talk," the last thing you want to do is to hear Kalindi's voice – because you know that if you hear Kalindi, you are going to probably listen to Kalindi.

Gourasana used to say that. There is a talk from Gourasana where He says that when you are in your illusion, or not happy with the path, or your transformation, the last thing you want to do is come toward Kalindi. Because coming toward Kalindi will be the truth, and will be the love, and you won't want that. You have decided to take yourself away from God.

Notes:

Of course, that is not what you will say. You will say, "I'm not taking myself away from God. I have God," as angry or stubborn as you may be in your fight for your life.

Some people need to just be left alone because that is how they go through the process of getting through their illusion, and that is okay. But, when you are in that place, I would recommend to grab for this talk. Grab for it, because all you need to do is wake up, be aware, and get your connection. But that illusion is so strong and just covers you over so strongly. If you can just scream for Gourasana, just get that out of your mouth, just "Gourasana" one time: "Gourasana, help!" Just like that, and remember your connection with Him.

You are going to become stronger if you practice this practice that I'm telling you about of being in a higher consciousness, being aware and awake. You won't go so far in a ditch with your illusion anymore if you practice this. You are going to become more awake now, and more aware, and more connected. You are just not going to be so sleepy in the illusion that you will even get covered over that much. You will have a way out more easily. But you will fall off the path. But now you have a way out of the illusion, and something to do that will pull you out very fast and help you regain your awareness. As soon as you regain your awareness, you will defeat the illusion.

Notes:

_____

_____

_____

As soon as you realize you are off the path, start preaching the truth to yourself, preach it out loud to yourself; or listen to my talk or do whatever you need to do to get yourself out of that illusion. Don't hang around in it! Don't stay in it! Look at the books that I have given you. *Let go, give up, surrender.* Remember your desire. And remember: "Oh, I forgot, I'm off the path. Oh, my God, how did I do that? Oh, my God, I can't believe it. I went off the path just for one day, and here I am out here, lost and crazed. I have to become awake – I have to get that talk. I have to listen to Kalindi and wake up!"

Notes:

The Power of Choice – Change Your Mind

Spoken on October 10, 2006

The power of choice is that you can change your mind!

All day long, you make choices and you change your mind. You change your mind constantly. I want everyone to change your mind in a certain way. (I always want 100 people to change when I am speaking about something new that needs to happen, because I believe in the "Hundredth Monkey*" theory.) I want at least 100 people to change their minds with the power of choice: change your mind from negative thinking to positive thinking, and live every day with a positive attitude.

I want you to change to positive thinking, because we are going to be in the material world anyway, and whatever is going to happen is going to happen anyway. We have been

---

* The *Hundredth Monkey Effect* is a theory based on a story in which a new behavior of a group of monkeys on one island spread to many, many monkeys on other islands once 100 monkeys started doing it.

Notes:

blessed over and over to have a type of life from which you can look at the rest of the world and see so many people are not so blessed. We have a place to live, we have food to eat, and it is possible to get a job. And on top of that, we are blessed to find a spiritual path leading to God, to the love of God, to the love of humankind, and to the love of self. And we are able to do something in this life to help humankind and to serve God in such an incredible way that it is going to make a difference in this world, an ongoing difference. What an incredible thing to live for; what an incredible thing to wake up for every day and to thank God for another day.

Are there hard times? Of course there are hard times. But you can choose to live a negative life or a positive life amidst the hard times. You can be having a very difficult time, and you can either have a positive outlook about it or a negative outlook about it.

The positive outlook is going to cause you to stand up strong and to be a good influence to yourself and to others. It is going to make your life a whole lot better, because you are going to be here in this material world and going through your transformation, which I know is very, very difficult; and you are going through life, which involves suffering. There is no way around it. Transformation is a very, very rough road. But thank God you have found the road to transformation. Thank God you have found your way to God. Thank God

Notes:

_____

_____

_____

you can help people. Thank God, thank God, thank God, that you can wake up another day!

The power of choice is just a matter of changing your mind. You have to put your whole self behind it and just say, "I am just going to change my mind." That is the power of choice.

We have a lot to be grateful for, and that gratitude should be shown by living a positive, creative, and productive life.

You can find whatever it is that allows you to shift and change your mind. It really is that simple. It's like, "Wait a minute here, I'm going to change that way of thinking."

Because you have a habit of being negative, it might take a week to wake up and say, "It can be hard. I am having a tough time today." You can still live with a positive attitude. "Yeah, that was a tough day at work today." So, it was a tough day at work. So what?

I will tell you a story now that has permanently changed my mind. There is a woman in the Philippines that has very, very, bad, bad, bad, bad crippling arthritis in her hands – you can imagine that kind of pain. She also has two little children and she is a single mother. The only job she can find is to scrub floors. That is the way she feeds her children and takes care of her life – scrubbing floors every day and then coming home and taking care of her children. That story

Notes:

_____

_____

_____

was told to me by a good friend of mine, because my life is not easy. He was trying to tell me, "What are you going to do, Kalindi? This is how it is." When he told me that story, I just said, "Thank you," and I changed my mind about my life because I thought, "What can I say in the face of that story?"

I am grateful every day that I wake up; whatever I have to go through and whatever I have to face, so be it. I am so grateful to be able to help God, to help people to find their way to love in a world that has no love. I am so grateful, and all I want to do is just stay alive one more day and one more day and one more day. Life is life; it is not a bowl of cherries.

Look around and see how much you are being given. Don't focus on all of the bad things and how hard your transformation is and how hard everything is. Change your mind about it all. What is hard is hard. It is going to be hard whether you are negative or positive, and it is much easier to be someone who has a positive attitude. It is the best way to live, and it is the best way to go through this transformation. I am telling you now, you have the power of choice to do this, and it is the illusion that wants you to be down and out. I'm asking you to join me and change your mind to positive thinking.

Notes:

_____

_____

_____

Live, Love, and Let Go

Spoken on July 28, 2007

Every time you are letting go, you need to feel the greater happiness that you have because you did let go. You need to watch for that greater happiness and see how a burden has been lifted. Something is going to be better every time you let go. If you can understand that, then maybe you can understand living your life in a "let-go state."

Live your life in a let-go state. That is how you should be living in order to come into the light more and more every day. *Come into the light and stay in the light.* You need to live in the light to stay in the light.

In order to stay in the light, you have to keep moving, keep saying "yes," and keep going forward. Otherwise you stop, and then what? The light is a constantly moving situation. When you stop, it's like you pull yourself out of the light until you make the decision to keep going. You could be stopped for months or years. So you want to keep letting go.

When there comes a big thing that is going to take some time to let go of, let go of all the little things around the big thing until you can muster up the strength to let go of the

Notes:

big thing. Just keep letting go so you can keep moving forward in the light. Have constant greater awareness and constant connection. Don't ever come out of your connection. Stay in your connection all of the time.

When you are working through the darkness, do not do it without being in your connection. Do not walk away from the light. Do not walk away from God when you are working through your darkness. That is a very big mistake. Cling to God's hand when you are working through your darkness; you cling onto God like never before. Do not ever go into the dark world of illusion and try to leave God behind. Stay with God, now that you have God so much. Never leave Him, ever. That is your part as a seeker of the Lord. Once you have found Him, you have to keep looking His way, stronger and stronger and stronger; hold on to Him tighter and tighter instead of holding on to the illusion so strongly.

So wake up again. This is just a wake-up call. Do not go into the darkness or go to play in the illusion and try to leave God behind. Take hold of God's hands and start to pull on them, and just keep pulling. Crawl toward Him more and more until He is holding you firmly and you are no longer going to play in the illusion.

If you are someone who wants to go Home, ask Him, "Please, I do not want my false self anymore. I do not want

Notes:

the being of illusion anymore. Please take it away. I give my free will back to You. Please, Father, take me Home." That is a basic prayer for someone who wants to go Home. If you don't want to go Home, watch out what you pray for. Pray for exactly what it is that you do want, and God is going to help you with what your true desire is. But either way, start letting go and living in that let-go state. It is the only way to live. It is the only way to bring peace and harmony around you in this material place.

Live, love, and let go.

Notes:

IT'S GOD THAT IS HAPPENING

There comes a point in your progress where you can let go at a very rapid rate. One may endeavor for ten years and seem to not make so much progress, and then in the eleventh year, give up 80 percent of their material activities. And then be moving so fast that they can see, as you say, the light at the end of the tunnel. They can see that it is possible.

GOURASANA

So What?

Spoken on February 19, 2008

To conclude the Break-Free Message talk series, I want to tell you a story about a conversation that Gourasana had with The Lady.

There was a period in the very beginning, during the years with the Core before the Mission started, when the Core was working in meditation every day for quite some time: maybe a couple of years. We were going deep, going deep, going deep, going deep, and just wrestling with the demons inside and with the illusion. We were just going deeper and deeper and deeper, and it felt like there just was no end. During the day, things were building inside of us, and during the night we would meditate. The Lady asked, "Gourasana, how long are we going to be meditating like this and doing the work like this?" And Gourasana said, "So what if it is for the rest of your life?" Of course, there was nothing said back to Gourasana, because The Lady knew that what He meant was, "You are getting God, you are finding the Lord, and of course you will do anything; and if it is that you have to meditate like this for the rest of your life, so be it."

Notes:
_____

_____

_____

There were no issues going on. The meditating was so deep that there couldn't be an issue; there could only be letting go.

So once again – I know I've said this many times – but *the only solution to the problem that you may be having is to go deeper,* whether it is deeper in your meditation or whether it is deeper in your consciousness.

When you go deeper, your issues cannot go with you. The issues are on the surface. And when you drop deeper, your issues cannot go with you because you dropped to a more real, true place within, more connected with God. The issues don't go to that depth with you. When you get to that depth, then you can do the real work.

You also need to remember to always work on the bigger things. Work on the bigger things; don't work on the little things. If you can do this, then all the small issues that seem so important will just fall away when you tackle the bigger things.

Sometimes there is not anything to work on. Sometimes you just need to sit in meditation and just go deep; just sit and go deep and then go deeper and deeper and deeper.

You will be with the Lord in your depth. You will learn to go very, very deep. When you find Him at that depth and you just are with the Lord, it is so sweet. The Lord will

Notes:

show you and tell you what you need to do when you go so deep. He is going to help you, but you have to go deep to connect to Him.

Your intuition is not Him. I talk lightly of going deep and being with Him, but being with Him is a very deep situation. I want to warn you in some way not to take the going within lightly. He is just going to be with you. You need to get there. You need to go so deep to find Him. But when you find Him, it is going to be the sweetest thing to just be able to sit in your depth with the Lord.

Notes:

You Are
On Your Way

Spoken on August 16, 2007

The spiritual work that you have been doing has been the work of breaking free of the illusion, of breaking up all of the illusion inside of you. *You are on your way.* I just want to explain to you what it is that you are doing and how much more there is to go through. And I want to let you see the bigger picture of what you have to go through.

I would like us not to talk so much about breaking free, but rather that everybody is getting freer and freer every day and closer and closer to the endless love of God in their spiritual transformation. We are all doing it together. There are those that are striving to break the cycle of birth and death, and there are certain programs that they are doing and certain ways that they are living their lives in order to accomplish that, but they are also getting freer and freer and closer and closer to the endless love of God every day.

The common link of getting freer and closer to love of God every day needs to be acknowledged. The people who are trying to break free may not make it. If someone

Notes:

239

asks, "What was that spiritual work all about?" Well, they got so much freer and so much closer to the love of God. We all need to become a team, together, because we have such a big job to do. Some people will make it to freedom and some people won't, but together we have such a big job to do. We all need to put all of our effort forward, together, toward the job that has to be done in this world. There is a big job to do in this world, and we are going to do our part.

Everything that you think you are, is going to die; and while it is dying, you are being filled with love and light. With that love and light, you are going to help so many people. All of you are going to help so many people.

Breaking the cycle of birth and death is not something that you necessarily will understand during the first years of your transformation. That is why it is so important that I want to talk about the Path as a path of the love of God and getting freer and freer every day, closer and closer to God every day. And there is a path to ultimate freedom, guided by Kalindi who specifically offers the guidance for people that know they want to return Home in this lifetime – no rebirth. This has to be stated so that people can go in that direction if they want to.

As you dive deeper and deeper into the Path and as your ego starts to die more and more and you become filled with more light and more truth, you will come to under-

Notes:

stand so much more than you do now. This will be true all
the way through your path, as you continue to be filled with
more and more light and awareness, and as you break free
out of the material realm.

Questioning everything is a part of the path Home;
it is part of the path to enlightenment. True enlightenment
is to take no more birth, no rebirth. The philosophy of no
rebirth cannot be understood; it can only be known through
faith, that somehow in your heart you know that there is
such a thing as rebirth. You just know it. You just come to
know it, and you know this is your last lifetime. It is not
something that you can fight in a debate and win. "Well,
how do you know that there is rebirth?" You know it in your
heart; you know it is true from your faith, but you do not
know from any kind of scientific proof that there is such a
thing as rebirth.

There are so many philosophies in the world, so why
have you chosen a path and a spiritual master that can help
you to take no rebirth? Because that is what you want. How
do you know that is what you want? Because that is what
you feel inside and know to be true, and that is the only
way that it can be explained. How do you know there is a
God? How do you know there is a Home? Because when
you start to go within, you start to feel God and you start to
feel Home. It is experiential. It is not from the mind.

Notes:

As you go forward in your transformation, faith is all you have to stand on. None of my explanations will carry you; you will only be able to stand on your direct experience of what you know in your heart.

Don't ever worry about trying to explain Home and God to somebody. If there is a debate going on, you have to back out, because the only thing you know is what you know from your heart. You can just say, "I can feel in my heart that there is birth after birth. And I know that there is the Lord, because I have felt the Lord. And I know that there is a Home, because I have felt Home. And I know the direction I am going in. And I know about the ego and the being of illusion, because I can feel mine disappearing."

Good luck. Call on Gourasana. When you are calling on Gourasana, you are calling on Gourasana within the Host. It is the Lord, it is Gourasana within the Host, not Gourasana that was in the body. Gourasana in the body was the Incarnation on earth that came through David Swanson. That is not where to put your focus; put your focus on Gourasana at the head of the Host. When you call on Gourasana, the head of the Host, you call the whole Host toward you. That force, that Incarnation from God, is here to help you so much.

If you are uncomfortable with calling on Gourasana, you can call on Kalindi, and the Host is still going to come

Notes:

racing to you. Maybe you will see and feel me by your side. Study all of these talks over and over again so that you can keep coming back to true yourself up to the teachings. The teachings are guidance to keep you going in the right direction on the Path, because you can easily get lost. My guidance for you will continue to come out.

Thank you for your transformation and for your continued transformation year after year. Thank you for giving and working on yourself and continually helping God's Mission. We are all becoming freer and freer and closer and closer to the endless love of God every day. I love you all so much. I hold you in my heart. I hold you in my arms.

Notes:

_____

_____

_____

Gourasana, "The Golden One," is a current-day Incarnation of God who came directly from the Source and manifested on this earth in 1987. He guided a small group of people, the "Core," to spiritual freedom. With His help, two of these people, Kalindi and The Lady, achieved a state of full awareness, spiritual freedom, and true enlightenment. They are spiritual masters for the world and Gourasana's successors. Gourasana's work was complete in 1995. He no longer walks this earth, but His energy, love, and presence are abundant and available.

Kalindi was given the special destiny to personally present spiritual truth to people who want to hear it, as the living Voice of God. As such, she founded the *Path to Ultimate Freedom*, in 1991. Since that time, she has been guiding this path to spiritual freedom and awakening spiritual masters. She has been delivering teachings and programs to help thousands of people to become freer and freer of the illusion each day and to come closer and closer to the endless love of God. The Path is part of Miracle of Love.

Miracle of Love is a nonprofit, nondenominational church that has a worldwide network of centers and communities. Programs, teachings, books, lectures, DVD's, Internet classes and personal loving support are provided for people traveling the path Home. Anyone, anywhere in the world can become a student or disciple of Kalindi.

One of the main offerings is the *Miracle of Love Seminar*, offered throughout the world. This is a profound six-day experience guiding people within to wake up their consciousness, discover the truth of who they are, and experience unconditional love – a personal, undeniable connection to God. Participants are guided within to do their spiritual work, finding release from pain, fear, guilt, shame, anger, heartbreak, etc. In the Seminar, they learn the Modern-Day Meditation.

The Modern-Day Meditation is a unique meditation practice, which provides direction for achieving both spiritual and material success. This meditation was first named the *Gourasana Meditation Practice* (or *GMP*) after Gourasana, who developed it. It is designed to help with all aspects of modern living, including the needs of body, mind, heart, and spirit. The Modern-Day Meditation is also referred to as the "Meditation for This Age." "This age" stands for the next 2,000 years of awakening.

Gourasana: Translates to mean "the Golden One." He is a current-day Incarnation of God. He comes directly from the Source.

David Swanson: The man who allowed his body to be used for Gourasana to come into the world from 1987 until 1995, at which time the body died.

Kalindi: A fully realized spiritual master for the world; Gourasana's first disciple and His successor, along with The Lady.

The Core: The group of seven people who Gourasana worked with when He first came. They include Kalindi, The Lady, Jim St. James, Mazzarati B. Mata, Marie, Candy (formerly Cindy), and Maha.

The Mission: The general term used to describe the varied forms of assistance being given as a direct result of Gourasana's coming to earth. Sometimes used to refer to Miracle of Love, a nondenominational church and the principal organization formed to accomplish His mission. (See "Origins of Miracle of Love," above.)

The Heavenly Host of light beings: Also called "the Host," "light beings," and "true selves." It is a large group of spiritual beings that came with Gourasana to help the people who want to leave this material realm and return Home. When Gourasana spoke, he often referred to Himself along with this group as "We" or "Us." The presence of this group helps make it possible for Gourasana to bring in so much power, so much special assistance, and so much love into the planet.

True self: The soul, the part of spirit that is always connected to God.

The path: A "path" is each person's personal spiritual path.

The Path: The "Path" sponsored by Miracle of Love is a spiritual path to ultimate freedom (currently called Path to Ultimate Freedom, although the name has changed over time) founded by Kalindi based on Gourasana's teachings. The Path is a way to participate in Miracle of Love; it is designed to help people break the cycle of birth and death in this lifetime, and to help people come closer to the love of God and get freer and freer from the illusion every day.

The illusion: Refers to the material realm, the plane of existence of which the earth is a part. It also is used to refer to the actual force of darkness that works against you.

The ego: Illusion within a person; parts of the illusory self that cover over the true self. The ego is the false self, illusory self: that part of a person that is not real.

The true realm of existence: Also called the "true realm" or "Home." It refers to the spiritual realm or the spiritual plane of existence. The spiritual plane is where the spirit soul resides with God.

Breaking the cycle of birth and death: Refers to returning Home to God, taking no more birth. This spiritual state can only be achieved while a person is alive. Then at the natural time of death of the body, the soul fully returns Home. Kalindi also calls this "ultimate union with God."

Sometimes Kalindi calls this *true* enlightenment, because the term "enlightenment" is often misused.

Modern-Day Meditation: also called Gourasana Meditation Practice (GMP), the "Meditation for This Age." This meditation has four parts or components. The components are opening the emotional body, calming, thinking, and going into action. When Kalindi says, "hit the floor," she is referring to meditating using the GMP; it is common to start the meditation practice by sitting on the floor. When Kalindi talks about screaming or crying in meditation, she is referring to Part One of the meditation, which often happens through opening the emotional body.

The Miracle of Love Seminar: Although this event changes and evolves over time, at the printing of this book, this is a six-day event. In this event, you are given an opportunity to uncover a profound connection to God and your true self. (See Origins of Miracle of Love, above, and the Contact Information on the last page to get further information.)

God, Source, Spirit, Father, Everything: Kalindi uses many different names to refer to the Supreme Almighty. Although Kalindi often refers to God in the masculine, this reference is not meant to limit any notion of God's form or name or gender.

Special assistance: Due to the unusually large number of souls that want to return Home at this time, this is specific spiritual help from this Incarnation of God, Gourasana, and the Heavenly Host, who have come explicitly to help people who are asking for it to break the cycle of birth and death in this lifetime. The transformational energy is a part of the special assistance. The special assistance is coming forth to help individuals in many different kinds of ways in order to help them move forward at a rapid enough speed to be able to succeed in the transformation; the speed of transformation has never been as fast as this. The special assistance is also working night and day all over the world in a global effort to help all of humankind with the predicament that is holding back love. And there are many ways this special assistance is holding back terrible things from happening on this earth.

Transformational energy: The benevolent spiritual power from God through the Host to help you break free of illusion. This energy started in the 1960's; it is available throughout the world in full power now and is starting to spread around the world. Gourasana let it be known how to work with this energy, as well as how to understand the special assistance and how to work within that energy.

We wish to express our heartfelt thanks to the many people for whom the publication of *The Break-Free Message* was a labor of love.

Kalindi's words were reviewed, assembled, and edited by Tamara La Toto, Kendra Davis, and Nan Inglis. Special thanks to Ed Jerum for help with the words of Gourasana and The Lady. Thank you to Jennifer Luth and Claus Pfitzner for design, Dirk Gräßle for layout and Leslie McDonald for production.

For more information, contact us at:

www.miracle.org
www.gourasana.org
www.miracleofloveseminar.org
www.theladyinprayer.org

US main number
(800) 338-3788

Los Angeles
(866) 922-3366

Asheville, NC
(888) 250-8115

Germany
++49 [0]180-Kalindi
++49 [0]180-525 46 34

Holland
++31 [0]88-Miracle
++31 [0]88-6472 53

Switzerland
+44 586 0730

Australia
+61 8 9284 5104

Argentina
00 54 11 5983 0981

Audio versions of Kalindi's talks are available for purchase at
www.bookstore.miracle.org